Personal Bankruptcy

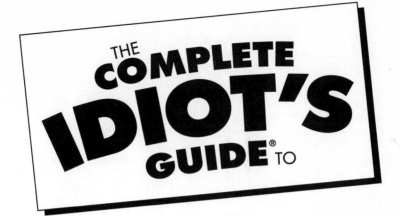

Personal Bankruptcy

by Lita Epstein, MBA

ALPHA

A member of Penguin Group (USA) Inc.

3 3113 02933 6536

ALPHA BOOKS

Published by the Penguin Group

Penguin Group (USA) Inc., 375 Hudson Street, New York, New York 10014, USA

Penguin Group (Canada), 90 Eglinton Avenue East, Suite 700, Toronto, Ontario M4P 2Y3, Canada (a division of Pearson Penguin Canada Inc.)

Penguin Books Ltd., 80 Strand, London WC2R 0RL, England

Penguin Ireland, 25 St. Stephen's Green, Dublin 2, Ireland (a division of Penguin Books Ltd.)

Penguin Group (Australia), 250 Camberwell Road, Camberwell, Victoria 3124, Australia (a division of Pearson Australia Group Pty. Ltd.)

Penguin Books India Pvt. Ltd., 11 Community Centre, Panchsheel Park, New Delhi—110 017, India

Penguin Group (NZ), 67 Apollo Drive, Rosedale, North Shore, Auckland 1311, New Zealand (a division of Pearson New Zealand Ltd.)

Penguin Books (South Africa) (Pty.) Ltd., 24 Sturdee Avenue, Rosebank, Johannesburg 2196, South Africa

Penguin Books Ltd., Registered Offices: 80 Strand, London WC2R 0RL, England

International Standard Book Number: 978-1-59257-947-1
Library of Congress Catalog Card Number: 2009930706

12   11   10   8   7   6   5   4   3   2   1

Interpretation of the printing code: The rightmost number of the first series of numbers is the year of the book's printing; the rightmost number of the second series of numbers is the number of the book's printing. For example, a printing code of 10-1 shows that the first printing occurred in 2010.

Printed in the United States of America

Note: This publication contains the opinions and ideas of its author. It is intended to provide helpful and informative material on the subject matter covered. It is sold with the understanding that the author and publisher are not engaged in rendering professional services in the book. If the reader requires personal assistance or advice, a competent professional should be consulted.

The author and publisher specifically disclaim any responsibility for any liability, loss, or risk, personal or otherwise, which is incurred as a consequence, directly or indirectly, of the use and application of any of the contents of this book.

Most Alpha books are available at special quantity discounts for bulk purchases for sales promotions, premiums, fund-raising, or educational use. Special books, or book excerpts, can also be created to fit specific needs.

For details, write: Special Markets, Alpha Books, 375 Hudson Street, New York, NY 10014.

Publisher: *Marie Butler-Knight*
Editorial Director: *Mike Sanders*
Senior Managing Editor: *Billy Fields*
Senior Acquisitions Editor: *Paul Dinas*
Development Editor: *Julie Bess*
Production Editor: *Kayla Dugger*

Copy Editor: *Krista Hansing Editorial Services, Inc.*
Book Designer: *Trina Wurst*
Cover Designer: *Bill Thomas*
Indexer: *Angie Bess*
Layout: *Brian Massey*
Proofreader: *John Etchison*

Contents at a Glance

Contents

Appendixes

Introduction

As you think about filing for bankruptcy, you're likely facing a whirl-wind of emotions. Maybe you're ashamed at the financial position you're in and you're afraid your friends and family members will find out. Maybe you fear facing a bankruptcy trustee or judge to discuss your financial situation. Maybe you're wondering how your job could be impacted by your filing for bankruptcy. And you're probably thinking you'll never have a normal financial life after bankruptcy.

But you also may be relieved because a huge weight has been lifted off your shoulders—you won't have to worry about harassing telephone calls from creditors once they know you've filed for bankruptcy.

You're not alone with this mix of emotions. Many people face bankruptcy after a job loss, a medical emergency, or a divorce. Those are the three most common reasons people find the need to file for bankruptcy.

So the big question is, what will your life be like after bankruptcy? In this book, I take you through the basics of filing for bankruptcy—and then I talk about how to get back to your life after bankruptcy.

Bankruptcy can give you a financial fresh start and actually make your life easier once you've gotten your debts discharged. You will have to do some work cleaning up your credit history and gradually restoring your ability to access credit. But you can do it. In about three to four years after bankruptcy, if you make enough money, you can likely buy a house and a car. So don't worry—your financial life isn't over when you file for bankruptcy.

How We've Organized the Book

You'll start your journey into the depths of filing for bankruptcy by looking at the basics of bankruptcy. Then we get down to the nitty-gritty of the bankruptcy types and what is required to file Chapter 7 and Chapter 13 consumer bankruptcies. (We don't delve deeply into filing for business bankruptcy.) Then we take a look at what happens to your debt after bankruptcy and how you can use bankruptcy to save your key assets. Finally, we look at how to get your financial life back together after bankruptcy.

We've organized the book into four parts:

Part 1, "Bankruptcy Basics," explores the different types of bankruptcies, reviews which type of bankruptcy you can qualify for, and talks about the professionals you may want to contact before and during your bankruptcy filing.

Part 2, "Understanding the Bankruptcy Process," takes you through the nitty-gritty of what you need to know before filing for bankruptcy and then walks you through the actual process of filing for bankruptcy.

Part 3, "Using Bankruptcy for Specific Goals," shows you how you can use bankruptcy to save your home, get a fresh financial start, clear out medical debt, and clean up a financial mess after a divorce.

Part 4, "Life After Bankruptcy," shows you how to repair your credit history after bankruptcy, explores job issues you may face when you file bankruptcy, talks about how you can go about buying a car and a house again after bankruptcy, and reviews how to handle credit with your spouse, especially if only one of you filed for bankruptcy.

Extras

We've developed a few helpers you'll find in little boxes throughout the book:

def•i•ni•tion

These help you learn the language of bankruptcy.

 Debt Dangers

These give you warnings about missteps to avoid.

Bankruptcy Lore

These explore in greater depth some basics about bankruptcy and its history.

 Credit Cleaners

These give you tips to ease your process of filing for bankruptcy and recovering from bankruptcy.

Acknowledgments

I'd like to give a special thanks to Paul Dinas, my acquisitions editor. I'd also like to thank my other editors at Alpha Books for all their help in making this book the best it can be—Julie Bess, development editor, and Krista Hansing, copy editor. Finally, I want to thank my husband, H. G. Wolpin, whose support helps me keep going especially when I'm on deadline.

Special Thanks to the Technical Reviewer

The Complete Idiot's Guide to Personal Bankruptcy was reviewed by an expert who double-checked the accuracy of what you'll learn here, to help us ensure that this book gives you everything you need to know about bankruptcy. Special thanks are extended to Guy W. Gupton, III, Esq.

Trademarks

All terms mentioned in this book that are known to be or are suspected of being trademarks or service marks have been appropriately capitalized. Alpha Books and Penguin Group (USA) Inc. cannot attest to the accuracy of this information. Use of a term in this book should not be regarded as affecting the validity of any trademark or service mark.

Chapter 1

What Is Bankruptcy?

In This Chapter

- Seeking a fresh financial start
- Why consider bankruptcy?
- Exploring bankruptcy types

Do you feel like you're drowning in debt and keep digging a deeper financial hole? Maybe you lost your job, faced a medical emergency involving a family member, went through a divorce, or lost a court case. Whatever caused your personal tragedy and led to the financial mess you're in, you just want to find a way to start over financially.

Bankruptcy might be the answer you're looking for. In this chapter, I review the basics of bankruptcy law in this country and compare it to that of other countries. I then explore the various reasons people choose to file for bankruptcy and briefly look at the types of bankruptcies you can file.

Bankruptcy for a Fresh Financial Start

American bankruptcy law provides a compassionate financial fresh start, even the most recent version that tipped the scales in favor of creditors. It's also far less punitive than the bankruptcy laws of other countries. You may get threatening phone calls from creditors who say they're going to file a lawsuit and have you jailed, but they can't do that in the United States unless they can prove credit fraud.

U.S. law includes no jail-time provision for people who fail to pay their credit cards, mortgages, or related debt. The one exception to this rule is ex-spouses who fail to pay child support or alimony; in these cases, you can be put into jail for failing to pay. Similarly, if someone can prove that you acted fraudulently in charging up that debt, you could be charged with consumer fraud. But as long as you didn't rapidly acquire debt with the intent to never pay, you can't be thrown in jail.

In some states, if you've stolen or forged a credit card or used a credit card that has been revoked or canceled, you can be charged with theft by deception. Also, if you charged an item and you never had the intention to pay for it or the ability to meet all your debt obligations, the issuer of the card can try to make a case for theft by deception. If a theft by deception case is made successfully, you can go to jail.

Luckily for us in the United States, the roots of bankruptcy law follow the lead of the Bible. The Old Testament calls for debt to be forgiven every seven years: "Everyone who has lent money to his neighbor is to cancel the debt; he must not try to collect the money; the Lord himself has declared the debt canceled." Jesus, too, preached debt forgiveness.

The first country to enact a bankruptcy law with the concept of debt forgiveness was England, in 1705. But the debtor had to get the consent of the creditor, and anyone who filed for bankruptcy fraudulently faced the death penalty. Before that law, Britain viewed debtors as criminals. Under a 1570 bankruptcy law, debtors were imprisoned, and their assets were seized and divided among creditors. If a debtor refused to cooperate, his ears could be cut off.

> ### Bankruptcy Lore
>
> Some countries do have debtors' prisons. Others, in the long-distant past, hacked up their debtors (early Romans). In medieval times, Italian creditors broke the bench or table of debtors so they couldn't continue their business. Robert Morris, who signed the Declaration of Independence, spent three years in debtors' prison in Britain before coming to America.

Today's more compassionate law did not come into play until 1978. Before that time, a struggle played out between debtors seeking relief and creditors wanting all their money back.

Let's take a look at how bankruptcy law has evolved in this country. The first formal laws in the United States date back to the uniformity clause of the constitution in 1787. Prior to that time, every state was free to disregard bankruptcy discharges granted by other states. As in England, debtors' prisons did exist in the United States. Finally in 1833, the federal government abolished debtors' prisons.

Bankruptcy law first started to consider the rights of debtors when Daniel Webster helped to push through the Bankruptcy Act of 1841. With that law, the United States clearly established that bankruptcy law must balance the interests of debtors and creditors, and not just be written purely to satisfy the needs of creditors. Several times between 1841 and 1978, when modern bankruptcy law was passed, creditors won over debtors and squashed any law that gave rights to debtors.

The most equitable bankruptcy law was passed in 1978, but the creditors weakened that law in 2005 with the passage of the Bankruptcy Abuse Prevention and Consumer Protection Act. Debtors have to jump through more hoops to file bankruptcy, and it is much more expensive for them to do so. But those who earn less than the median income for their household size within their state of residence can still do so. Those who earn more than that median income would flunk the first part of the "means test" (see Chapters 5 and 6), but might yet pass the second part, which is extremely complicated.

With the United States in an economic crisis in 2009, with millions of people losing their jobs, the bankruptcy law will likely be revisited to soften some of the harsher provisions of the 2005 act. The change that affects all people who file for bankruptcy relates to a test of income called the means test. We show you how that test impacts your bankruptcy filing in Chapters 5 and 6.

When you complete the requirements of bankruptcy court, your debts are discharged (with some exceptions) and you truly get a fresh financial start. Let's take a look at why people file bankruptcy.

When to Consider Bankruptcy

More than one million people filed for bankruptcy in 2008, which is an increase of more than 200,000 from the 2007 total filings of 801,140. Clearly, if you're thinking of filing for bankruptcy, you are not alone. In 2009, as unemployment levels rise, this number will go up even higher. So don't be embarrassed if you decide to file for bankruptcy this year or at some time in the future.

Why do people file? The most common reasons are job loss and medical emergency, but divorce also can wreak havoc on an otherwise stable financial situation. In addition, people use the bankruptcy code to stop foreclosure on their home, halt the repossession of a car, erase certain legal judgments, and halt seizures by the IRS. You can't erase *secured debt* with bankruptcy other than by giving up the secured property, but you can wipe out most, if not all, of your *unsecured debt*.

def•i•ni•tion

> **Secured debt** is debt for which you have put up an asset to back that debt. For example, when you take out a mortgage on your house, you secure the debt with your home. If you don't pay the debt, the bank can foreclose on your home.
>
> **Unsecured debt** is debt that is not backed by an asset. For example, most credit card debt and medical debt has no underlying asset securing that debt. If you can't pay, no asset can be seized and sold.

Just because you decide to file bankruptcy does not mean you intend to walk away from all your debts. Your repayment obligation depends on the type of bankruptcy you file and whether you want to reaffirm your debts with a *reaffirmation agreement.* In fact, by filing bankruptcy and getting rid of some of your unsecured debt, you may be able to afford the payments on your secured debt, such as those on your home or your car.

def•i•ni•tion

> You can choose to enter into a **reaffirmation agreement** with a creditor after filing bankruptcy but before receiving your discharge, and agree to repay the debt after the bankruptcy takes effect with receipt of the discharge.

Debt Relief from Unsecured Loans

If you're drowning in credit card debt, bankruptcy will erase most, if not all, of that debt. This can include hospital and doctor bills after a medical emergency. It can also include all your credit card bills, unless you used a credit card secured by a savings or checking account. In addition, personal loans that you took without an underlying asset can be wiped out with bankruptcy.

Whether you can wipe out all or part of the debt depends on the type of bankruptcy you file. I talk more about bankruptcy types later in the chapter.

Home Nearing Foreclosure

If your home is nearing foreclosure, you can file bankruptcy to halt that foreclosure. Whether you'll be able to keep the home in the long term will depend on whether you can get your mortgage up-to-date and then continue to pay it if you are filing Chapter 7. For those filing Chapter 13, you can work out a plan to repay any money past due (in arrears) as part of your repayment plan. Bankruptcy can't save your home if you can't pay the mortgage. For more on how to save a home using bankruptcy, read Chapter 8.

Car Could Be Repossessed

If you're parking your car in a different spot each night, hoping to hide it from the repo man, a bankruptcy filing can stop (temporarily in Chapter 7 and permanently in a workable Chapter 13) a repossession of your car. If the car has already been repossessed, you probably won't be able to get it back with a Chapter 7 filing, but you may be able to get it back with a Chapter 13 filing if it hasn't already been sold. I talk more about saving your car in Chapter 9.

Stop Hospitals and Doctors from Calling

If you have thousands in bills from doctors and hospitals that you just can't pay, bankruptcy can stop harassment and give you time to heal. Most, if not all, of this debt is likely unsecured, so you will be able to wipe it out as part of the bankruptcy. I talk more about medical debt in Chapter 10.

Need to Fix a Financial Mess After Divorce

Divorce creates a financial mess for everyone, but if you have a lot of debt from the marriage, the situation can be even more daunting. For example, you likely have bills to pay and disagreement over who is responsible for those bills. You may have a house to sell and have difficulty selling it, so you have to work out who will pay the mortgage. You may not want to sell the home so the children have some sense of security, but it's difficult to work out the finances for two households. In Chapter 11, I talk about the pitfalls of filing for bankruptcy after or before a divorce.

Erase Some Legal Judgments (but Not All)

Most of your court judgments can be discharged with the filing of a bankruptcy, but you must pay court-imposed fines and restitution, as well as back child support and alimony. You also can't erase debts owed because of a civil judgment from your willful or malicious acts, or for personal injuries or death caused by drunk driving. I talk more about the discharge of legal judgments in Chapters 5 and 6.

Halt IRS Seizures

You can stop IRS seizures of your property by filing a bankruptcy, but you won't be able to erase the so-called priority tax debt. Some federal and state tax debt cannot be erased, but your attorney may be able to negotiate with the IRS or the state tax authority for a settlement.

Stop the Loss of Your Driver's License

If you have unpaid judgments under the state insurance responsibility acts, you can use the Bankruptcy Code to prevent the revocation or suspension of your license. You can't erase the fines, but a bankruptcy filing can prevent the loss of your license to the extent that is traceable to a civil judgment rather than to a fine.

Prevent Garnishment of Your Wages

If a creditor won a suit in court and plans to garnish your wages, you can stop the garnishment by filing for bankruptcy. If the debt is unsecured and does get wiped out with bankruptcy, you won't have to repay the debt.

The Four Basic Types of Bankruptcy

The bankruptcy code defines four types of bankruptcy, but most individuals choose either Chapter 7 or Chapter 13. If your gross household income is above your state's median income based on household size, you may be forced to file under Chapter 13, but you'll undergo a means test to find out for sure (more on that in Chapter 5). The names for bankruptcy are drawn from the sections of the bankruptcy code related to each type of bankruptcy.

Businesspeople may file under Chapters 7, 11, or 13, but a corporation cannot file under Chapter 13. People who own or run a family farm or fishing business use Chapter 12. If your debt is primarily personal debt, you must use Chapter 7 or Chapter 13 even if you were running a business. Many people use personal credit cards to start up a new business, so the bankruptcy court will likely view the debt as primarily personal debt.

Let's take a closer look at the bankruptcy types.

Chapter 7

Chapter 7 allows you to liquidate, or wipe out, most of your debt. But to take advantage of this fresh start, you may have to give up some of your property. If you want to keep all of your property and repay some of your debt, be careful about using Chapter 7. Each state has different rules about what you can keep and what you can't.

Whether you'll be able to keep any of your assets depends on the exemptions in your state. You can find a brief list of those in Appendix C. I talk more about how this works in Chapter 5.

def•i•ni•tion

The bankruptcy court appoints a **bankruptcy trustee** to oversee your bankruptcy. This person seeks to find as much cash as possible to repay your creditors. This can include seizing assets and selling them.

In reality, people get to keep most of their personal possessions, such as clothes and furnishings, because the bankruptcy court can't collect a significant amount by selling it. Through its *bankruptcy trustee*, the court decides whether to sell your possessions to repay your creditors. One of the trustee's jobs is to gauge the likelihood of a meaningful recovery to creditors if your real and personal property were sold at auction. The trustee must determine whether the money made at auction will generate enough in profits to at least repay creditors some of the money that is due. An auction of used household items usually costs more than the amount of money that will be raised.

When your debts are discharged after a Chapter 7 bankruptcy, your slate is wiped clean and you don't owe anyone anything—unless, of course, you decided to reaffirm some of your debt, such as for your house or car. Some debts cannot be discharged. I talk more about what can and cannot be discharged in Chapters 5 and 6.

Chapter 13

Chapter 13 is a reorganization of your debt. You must develop a plan to repay at least part of your debt, and the bankruptcy court must approve this plan. The bankruptcy trustee will review your plan to recover as much as possible for your creditors.

You can develop a repayment plan to repay debts over three years or over five years. If you earn more than the median income, you will likely have to develop a five-year plan. When you file Chapter 13 bankruptcy, you file a plan to pay your so-called disposable earnings to the Chapter 13 trustee over a three- to five-year span. If your gross household income is above your state's median income based on your household size and you fail the means test, you must file a five-year plan. I talk more about this in Chapter 6.

During the time you are working through your repayment plan, the trustee controls your finances. If you want to sell any assets during that time, you can do so only with the approval of the trustee. Similarly, you make payments based on your repayment plan to the trustee, and he doles out those payments to the creditors according to the confirmed Chapter 13 plan.

If you successfully complete the payment plan, the remaining unsecured debt will be discharged. If you kept your house and car, you will still need to continue after discharge to make payments to keep your house, assuming that the mortgage did not pay out according to its terms in the course of the Chapter 13 case. I talk more about how Chapter 13 bankruptcy works in Chapter 6.

Chapter 11

Similar to Chapter 13, Chapter 11 is a reorganization of debt, but corporations and partnerships mostly use it. A Chapter 11 debtor usually proposes a plan of reorganization to keep the business alive and pay creditors over time. Individuals whose debts are primarily business debts can also file Chapter 11.

Debtors may "emerge" from a Chapter 11 bankruptcy within a few months or after several years. Unlike a Chapter 13 bankruptcy, which requires a minimum three-year repayment plan, the length of a Chapter 11 filing depends on the size and complexity of the bankruptcy.

Any interested party can propose a plan to get out of Chapter 11 bankruptcy. Creditors then vote for a plan. Upon its confirmation, the plan becomes binding. The plan should specify the treatment of debts and operations of the business for the duration of the plan. Either a "debtor in possession" or a bankruptcy trustee controls the finances of the company in Chapter 11 bankruptcy until the company emerges or dissolves.

While Chapter 11 bankruptcy is intended primarily for businesses, many celebrities and other wealthy individuals, such as doctors or lawyers, have filed under Chapter 11. People who have unsecured debts over $336,900 and secured debts over $1,010,650 in cases filed before April 1, 2010, must file for Chapter 11. (Those numbers change after that date.) Also, anyone who has substantial nonexempt assets, such as several pieces of real estate, must file under Chapter 11 instead of Chapter 13. Chapter 11 bankruptcy is more complex, and filing fees and legal fees are considerably higher.

The initial filing fee for a Chapter 11 bankruptcy is $839, compared to a filing fee of $299 for Chapter 7 and $274 for Chapter 13 bankruptcy. On top of that fee is a fee for disbursements of at least $250 per quarter; this can go as high as $10,000 per quarter when disbursements total $5 million or more. Many Chapter 11 bankruptcies end by a conversion to Chapter 7 bankruptcy as legal fees gobble up business assets.

Chapter 12

Chapter 12 bankruptcy is almost identical to Chapter 13, but it's intended for farmers and fishermen. To be eligible for Chapter 12, at least 80 percent of your debts must come from operating a family farm or fishing business. If you think you qualify for Chapter 12, consult your attorney for more details.

If you're not sure whether bankruptcy is the right move for you, you'll need to investigate your options. Let's start by looking at what you owe and what you own. Then we'll look at some alternatives to bankruptcy, to give you the full range of options.

The Least You Need to Know

- ◆ If you're drowning in debt, don't be embarrassed by filing for bankruptcy—it can give you a fresh financial start.

- ◆ How much you earn and how much you own impact the type of bankruptcy you can file.

- ◆ If most of your debts are personal debts and you want relief from them, you need to file for Chapter 7 or Chapter 13 bankruptcy.

- ◆ If most of your debts are business debts and you want relief from them, you have to file for Chapter 11 bankruptcy.

2

Is Bankruptcy Right for You?

In This Chapter

- ◆ Assessing your finances
- ◆ Looking at other fixes
- ◆ Determining eligibility

Bankruptcy may seem as though it's the perfect tool to get all those nasty creditors off your back and escape the daily harassing phone calls, but is it the right thing for you? You need to think about how it will impact your life and whether you would lose too much if you seek that escape from your financial troubles.

In this chapter, I help you look at what you owe and what you own. Then I review alternatives to bankruptcy. Next, I briefly review the eligibility requirements for each type of bankruptcy and talk about how bankruptcy can impact your life.

Road Map to Bankruptcy

The road to bankruptcy usually creeps up on you slowly as you move from financial crisis to financial crisis. Maybe you can't afford something you need or want, so you decide to put it on a credit card or take out a loan (those 0 percent loans look great until you have to pay them off).

All seems to be moving along smoothly. You're paying the bills on time, but the amount due slowly gets higher and higher. Then a major financial shock happens—you lose your job, you get sick and can't work, or your marriage beaks up, to name a few common reasons people face bankruptcy.

Credit Cleaners

Be sure to pull your credit reports from all three credit reporting agencies—Equifax, Experian, and TransUnion—before meeting with your bankruptcy attorney. You can do that for free at www.annualcreditreport.com.

Before you even talk with an attorney about the option of filing bankruptcy, you need to pull together some key information. Without these details, errors could be made in your bankruptcy filing. You may end up forgetting about a debt that could have been discharged, or you may forget that you are a part owner on something and be forced to sell it to satisfy creditors.

Listing What You Own

First, start by listing everything you own. If you could be listed as an owner of family-owned land or a family business, check into this before you file for bankruptcy. People have been forced to sell family-owned assets because they filed bankruptcy and didn't know their name was on the title to the land or on the business. Their parents made those arrangements but didn't discuss it with them.

While you may be embarrassed about having to file bankruptcy, you should discuss that possibility with family members and anyone else with whom you share assets. The bankruptcy court's first priority is to satisfy creditors, not to help you find a way to protect your assets.

If the bankruptcy trustee finds undisclosed assets that can be sold to help pay off your creditors, it likely will force the sale of those assets unless your state offers an exception or homestead exemption (see Appendix C for a state-by-state listing). Adding insult to injury, your failure to disclose may prevent you from taking an exemption that would otherwise have been available.

 Debt Dangers _____

List every debt and every asset you own—even if it's just a small share of a family business—before you meet with your attorney. Leaving out a debt could mean you still have to pay for it after the bankruptcy. Forgetting about an asset could result in losing that asset to a forced sale to pay creditors. Your discharge may even be put at risk if you forget to list an asset.

For example, suppose you filed for Chapter 7 bankruptcy and are part owner on a family plot of land worth $500,000. Your stake in that land is only $50,000. Since you don't live on the land, your state exemption may not protect it. The bankruptcy judge would likely force the sale of the land to get that $50,000 to help pay off creditors. If another family member couldn't come up with the cash, the land would have to be sold.

Your attorney needs to know about everything that might have your name on it. So don't worry about the embarrassment. Call your family members before filing for bankruptcy to be sure you are aware of all your assets.

If a family member is near death and you may get an inheritance, be sure to talk about this with your attorney. The 180-day look-forward period for inheritances could allow the bankruptcy court to take that inheritance, sell it, and use it to repay creditors even if the family member's death happens 179 days after the bankruptcy filing.

Use the following worksheet to help you sort out your assets.

Asset	Value
Real property	
Your home	
Other real property	
Timeshares	
Your cars	
Car you use for work	
Other vehicle	
Bank account balances	
Checking	
Savings	
Other	
Household goods	
Furniture	
Appliances	
Audio and video equipment	
Computers and accessories	
Other household items	
Art collectibles	
Jewelry	
Firearms	
Hobby equipment	
Stocks	
Bonds	
Other investments	
Cash value of life insurance	
Interests in any trusts (Be sure to check with family)	
Business interests (If there is a family business, be sure to check with family)	

Asset	Value
Money owed to you	
Alimony and support	
Bonuses due from work	
Commissions due	
Legal claims	
Tax refunds	
Life insurance payments due (beneficiary on a life insurance policy)	
Estate distributions that are expected after the death of a family member	
Patents and copyrights	
Tools and machinery used for work	
Cash value on pensions	
Office equipment not included in household goods	
Business inventory	
Business interests	
Other assets	

In addition to your assets, you need to detail any income you receive or expect to receive, as well as any deductions from that income. If you are married, you should total these items separately. In some states, it makes more sense to file for bankruptcy together. In others, it's to your advantage to file separately. Your attorney can help you make this decision, but he needs the details about all income you receive. Use the following chart to gather key income information.

Income Source	Your Income	Your Spouse's Income	Total
Current gross wages, salary, and commissions			
Estimated overtime pay			

continues

Income Source	Your Income	Your Spouse's Income	Total
Gross income from business, profession, or farm			
Gross income from rental properties			
Social Security and other government assistance			
Retirement income			
Other income			

You also should list any deductions that are taken out of your paycheck. Use the following chart to gather that information.

Payroll Deduction	You	Your Spouse	Total
Payroll taxes			
Social Security			
Medicare			
Insurance			
Union dues			
Pension contributions			
Repayments to pension loan			
Support payments deducted from check			
Other payroll deductions			

You can use this income detail to determine the types of bankruptcy you qualify for. I talk more about eligibility later in the chapter.

Acknowledging What You Owe

Your next big job is to list everything you owe. If you're like many people in debt, you probably don't know the details of all your debt or you may have forgotten some accounts. That's common. Once debt gets to a certain level, people prefer not to add it all up. But it's time to do that tally. If you forget something and don't put it on your bankruptcy filing, you could still owe the debt.

To be sure you've listed everything, get a copy of all three of your credit reports from the major credit-reporting agencies: Experian, Equifax, and TransUnion. In addition to this search, you should do a search of public records to be certain no one has filed a lien against you or your property or has filed a lawsuit to collect a debt. Your attorney can assist you with a public records search if you need the help.

Credit Cleaners

You can get your credit reports for free by going to the website www.annualcreditreport.com. Be sure you go back to this website as you request each one; don't get caught up in a monthly payment plan for credit monitoring. When you get to each agency's website, you'll find a link for a free credit report. It's usually at the bottom of the page when you get to the website for each agency.

Often you will find public records on your credit report, but they're not always accurate or complete. This information is not reported directly to credit agencies, as are your credit card accounts. Periodically, the information is collected for the credit bureaus, so errors or omissions can happen.

Use the following chart to pull together information about your debt that is secured by an asset, such as your home mortgage and car loan.

Asset	Total Owed	Monthly Payment	Market Value of Assets	Amount You're Behind in Payments
Home				
Other real estate				
Car				
Other assets				

Use the following chart to pull together your other debt information.

Type of Debt	Amount You Owe	Minimum Monthly Payment
Credit cards		
Student loans		
Medical bills		
Income taxes		
Judgments		
Child support and alimony		
Fines and restitution obligations		
Loans to friends and relatives		
Tax liens		

Available Cash to Repay the Debt

Now that you've got everything on paper, it's time to take a close look and see if there's any chance that you can repay the debt you've built up. First calculate your monthly income by using the information on your income chart. Then subtract deductions from your check. This will give you the amount of net cash you have each month to pay the bills.

Here's what that calculation should look like:

Total gross monthly income	$
Minus payroll deductions	($)
Total net cash	$

Next add up your monthly amount due on secured loans. Then add up the monthly amount due on your unsecured debt. Finally, subtract the amount of cash you make.

Here's what that calculation should look like:

Total monthly payments on secured debt	$
Total monthly payments on unsecured debt	$
Total monthly payments for all debt	$
Subtract total net cash	− $
Shortfall (surplus)	

If the number is a negative number, you have more cash than you need each month to pay the bills. This may not mean that you have enough to live on, but it does mean that if you can work with your creditors, you may be able to come up with a reasonable monthly budget, especially if you can get your creditors to lower your interest rates on some credit cards, thereby lowering the monthly payments. Credit counseling or debt consolidation may be options to consider. I talk more about that later in the chapter.

If you're drowning in debt and you owe more monthly than you make, you likely won't have any choice but to file for bankruptcy unless you can borrow money from friends or family. That's a difficult choice to make, and unless you have a very wealthy friend or family member who can wait a while for repayment, this is not an option to consider. Borrowing from family and friends and then not paying it back can be more hazardous to your long-term relationships than filing for bankruptcy; you could lose a friend or family member permanently over past-due debt. Think long and hard about whether you want to go down that path.

Bankruptcy vs. Other Credit Fixes

Should you consider another method of debt payment than filing bankruptcy? That depends on the type of debt you owe, whether you want to save assets, and how much cash you have to work with to come up with a fix other than bankruptcy. You need to ask yourself these two questions:

◆ Is the money I owe primarily on secured assets?

◆ Is the money I owe primarily for unsecured debts?

If the money you owe is primarily on secured assets, bankruptcy may or may not help you save them. You won't be able to keep the assets unless you reaffirm the debt and continue to pay for them. Even then, depending on the homestead exemptions and exceptions in your state (see Appendix C), the bankruptcy court could still sell those assets to satisfy creditors. A bankruptcy attorney can help you sort that out.

Bankruptcy can stop a foreclosure and give you time to work out arrangements so you can catch up on your payments. I talk more about how to save your house with bankruptcy in Chapter 8.

Credit Cleaners _____

If you're having trouble paying your mortgage, you can get free assistance from a HUD Housing Counselor. You can search online for a counselor near you at www.hud.gov/offices/hsg/sfh/hcc/hcs.cfm. Or you can call 1-800-569-4287 to find a Housing Counselor near you. Another good source for help is the Homeowner Crisis Resource Center of the NFCC, 1-866-845-2227. Also, under the Obama affordable homes plan, you can check out https://makinghomesaffordable.gov.

If what your owe is primarily for unsecured debts, you need to decide whether you want to pay down the debt or use bankruptcy to wipe it out. If you have a lot of assets that you want to save, bankruptcy may not be your best choice. The bankruptcy court's first priority will be satisfying your creditors, so if it sees assets that it can sell and generate cash to pay off your creditors, it will order the assets sold unless they are protected by your state's exemptions (see Appendix C).

If you do want to consider what options you have other than bankruptcy, I briefly discuss the pros and cons of these options shortly, including credit counseling, loan modification, debt consolidation, and debt settlement. All these options will lower your credit score, but they disappear from your credit reporting much sooner than bankruptcy. I talk more about life after bankruptcy in Part 4.

Credit Counseling

Credit counselors can help you negotiate better rates and payment options. This can help you pay down your credit card debts. If you're trying to save a house, you're better off working with a housing counselor, as mentioned previously.

 Credit Cleaners

If you decide to work with a credit counselor, be sure it's someone affiliated with the National Foundation for Credit Counseling (www.nfcc.org). You can search for a counselor near you online or by calling 1-800-388-2227.

Credit counselors offer a full range of services including advice on how to manage your money better, solutions for your current financial problems, and help in developing a personalized plan that you can use to prevent future difficulties. Good ones can offer you *debt-management plans*, money-management education, and homeowner counseling and education. Often these counselors not only help you come up with a plan for repaying your debt, but also contact your creditors and negotiate lower interest rates. Once these rates are in place, they help you develop a repayment plan so you no longer will get those harassing calls.

def•i•ni•tion

A **debt-management plan** is a systematic way to pay down your debt. For a debt-management plan to work, you need enough income to make the payments.

Credit counseling can be a good option if you definitely want to pay off all your debt, but be careful when contacting a credit counselor if you're sure you want to file bank-ruptcy. Talk with your attorney before contacting a credit counselor if you plan to file bankruptcy.

Credit counseling is the required first step before you can file for bankruptcy. There are some exceptions, which we discuss in Chapters 5 and 6, but even if you meet these exception requirements, you'll still need to see a credit counselor shortly after filing. You can find credit counselors that meet bankruptcy court requirements at www.usdoj. gov/ust/eo/bapcpa/ccde/cc_approved.htm.

While credit counseling exceptions do exist, harsh case law in this area shows you are much better off getting the counseling done prior to filing your bankruptcy case. Unless you're trying to save an asset and have no way to get a quick appointment with a counselor, take the time to comply with the credit counseling rule and don't file until at least one day after receiving credit counseling. Since you can do coun-seling by telephone and online, you shouldn't have a hard time getting a quick appointment.

Bankruptcy law as amended in 2005 (BAPCPA) requires credit coun-selors to determine whether you really need to file bankruptcy or whether an informal repayment plan would get you back in good financial shape. If your debts are too high and your income is too low, credit counseling may seem like a waste of time, but you don't have a choice.

Also, if you have a lot of credit cards with outrageous interest rates (more than 25 or 30 percent), with lots of penalties and late fees built up, or if you have a lot of medical bills or deficiency judgments (such as money due after the repossession of a car), credit counseling likely won't help you.

The law requires that you participate in credit counseling, but you don't have to go along with a repayment plan proposed by the credit-counseling agency. However, if the agency comes up with a repayment plan, you must file this repayment plan and your counseling certificate along with your other bankruptcy petition; that's why I highly recommend that you talk with your attorney before you go to credit counseling if you're certain that bankruptcy is your only option.

Debt Dangers

If a credit counselor believes you can complete a repayment plan, the court could use this as a reason to question a Chapter 7 filing and require you to file for Chapter 13 bankruptcy. You must submit the plan developed by a court-approved credit counselor. Some bankruptcy courts are more lenient and may not require you to file a debt-management plan. Check with your attorney for common practices locally.

Loan Modification

If you have very little credit card debt and your primary problem relates to your mortgage payments, a loan modification may be a good option for you. This could include extending the term of your loan (for example, from 30 years to 40 years), renegotiating your interest rate, or other options suggested by the loan servicer.

Loan modifications have been hard to get in the past, but in 2009, thanks to a major emphasis by the government on reducing foreclosures, you may find a loan modification easier to get. Your first step should be to call the people who collect your mortgage and tell them about your situation. If they can't help you, call one of the housing counselors mentioned previously.

Debt Consolidation

Consolidating your debt into one more affordable payment may be an option for you. You can find a debt-consolidation specialist at many different types of financial institutions, including your own bank. But be careful when considering debt consolidation.

If you consolidate your credit card debt to reduce your monthly payment, you will be converting unsecured debt (which can be discharged in a bankruptcy) to secured debt against your home. You may be putting your home at greater risk and just stalling the inevitable.

Consider a consolidation loan only if you truly plan to pay down that debt before starting to charge on your credit cards again. The costs of consolidation loans can also add up. You may have to pay points (1 percent of the amount you want to borrow) and other closing costs. However, these types of loans do offer a tax advantage because their interest is tax deductible, whereas the interest paid to credit card companies is not tax deductible.

Debt Settlement

Debt-settlement or debt-negotiation specialists focus solely on negotiating settlements with your creditors. While they're negotiating these pay-off settlements, they collect money from you on a monthly basis that will be used to pay your creditors when a settlement amount is reached.

Debt-negotiation specialists can be a very risky choice and can have a long-term negative impact on your credit report and your ability to get credit in the future. Fraudulent ones collect money and pocket it. Many states have laws regulating debt-negotiation companies and the services they offer. Before you sign a contract with a debt-negotiation company, contact your state attorney general for more information on the laws in your state. You can also check with the Better Business Bureau for information about the track record of the company you're talking to.

Are You Eligible?

After looking at these options, you may have decided that bankruptcy is your best bet. Next you'll need to know if you qualify.

Chapter 7

Generally, for Chapter 7 bankruptcy, your debts must be primarily consumer debts. Your gross household income needs to be below the median income for your state, based on your household size. The range can be as low as $16,950 for a family of two in Puerto Rico or as high as $101,941 for a family of five in Maryland.

Credit Cleaners

You can find out your state's median income at the Census bureau: www.census.gov/hhes/www/income/statemedfaminc.html. Download the spreadsheet to find the details of median income based on family size.

Even if your income is higher, you may pass the means test. I show you how to do a means test in Chapter 5.

Chapter 13

As long as the size of your debt falls within the limits of Section 109(e) of the Bankruptcy Code, you can use Chapter 13 bankruptcy. Your gross household income determines whether you can set up a three-year or five-year plan. If you complete the plan, all remaining unsecured debt (with certain exceptions located at Section 1328 of the Bankruptcy Code) will be *discharged* (erased).

If your unsecured debts are over $336,900 and your secured debts are over $1,010,650, you must file for Chapter 11 bankruptcy.

def•i•ni•tion

Discharge is a court order issued at the end of Chapter 7 or Chapter 13 bankruptcy that relieves a debtor of personal liability for debts that qualify.

Chapters 11 and 12

Chapter 11 and Chapter 12 bankruptcies primarily are used for business debts. Most businesses file under Chapter 11, but if your business involves family farming or fishing, you would use Chapter 12.

Wealthy individuals also file under Chapter 11 if they don't meet the Chapter 13 eligibility requirements.

How Bankruptcy Impacts Your Life

Initially, filing bankruptcy will take a huge weight off your shoulders because you'll be able to tell harassing credit callers that you filed bankruptcy and that they should now talk with the bankruptcy court; they can no longer call and harass you. You also can stop a home foreclosure and most other actions involving money you owe, as I discussed in Chapter 1.

While you're working with the bankruptcy court, that court will totally control your financial life. You won't be able to make any financial decisions without first contacting the court. In a Chapter 7 bankruptcy, this control could be for just a few months, but in a Chapter 13 bankruptcy, it will be true for at least three years—and possibly as long as five years.

After bankruptcy, when your case has successfully been completed, your debt will be discharged, except for that debt you reaffirmed. Initially, your credit will be in bad shape. The bankruptcy will stay on your credit report for 7 years after the debt is discharged for Chapter 13 bankruptcy, and 10 years for Chapter 7 or a dismissed Chapter 13. You may think Chapter 7 is worse, but in reality, since Chapter 13 takes three to five years to complete a repayment, Chapter 13 stays on your credit history for at least 10 years (possibly 12 years). I talk more about how to get your life back together after a bankruptcy in Part 4.

The next chapter takes a closer look at the key players you'll need to work with before and during bankruptcy filing.

The Least You Need to Know

◆ Carefully pull together all the details about your income and assets; this can greatly impact the type of bankruptcy you file and how much of your assets you get to keep.

◆ List all your debt; if it's not included in your bankruptcy filing, you'll still owe it.

◆ You may want to consider options to bankruptcy, but if you're drowning in debt, you probably won't have a choice.

◆ Your income level, your debt levels, and the source of the debt will impact the type of bankruptcy you can file.

Professionals You Should Contact

In This Chapter

- ◆ Counselors
- ◆ Financial advisors
- ◆ Debt-relief agencies

Filing for bankruptcy can be a scary prospect, but you won't be doing it alone. Professionals will assist you throughout the process. In this chapter, I discuss who they are and what help you should expect to get from them.

Role of Credit Counselors

Before you can file for bankruptcy, you must sit down with a credit counselor. This pre-bankruptcy counseling session must be with a counseling agency approved by the U.S. Trustee of the bankruptcy court.

The fee for this service generally is about $50. A typical counseling session lasts 60 to 90 minutes and can be done in person, on the telephone, or online. If you're filing an emergency bankruptcy petition (for example, to put a stay on a home nearing foreclosure), you can do this session after you file, as long as you complete it within 30 days after filing.

Even though you have the legal right to do this session after you file if you are filing an emergency petition, you should work exhaustively to get your credit counseling done before your case is filed.

Many of the credit counseling delays and bottlenecks of late 2005 have been eliminated, and with any patience you can get counseling done within a few hours of your first call or login. Your perseverance here is key, since very early after the 2005 bankruptcy law became effective, lawyers learned that very few cases can survive lack of pre-filing counseling.

Credit Cleaners

You can use the U.S. Trustee website to find the nearest counseling agency approved by the bankruptcy court: www.usdoj.gov/ust/eo/bapcpa/ccde/cc_approved.htm.

If you can't afford to pay a credit counselor, the counseling organization is required to provide the counseling free of charge. You must request a fee waiver from the counseling agency before the session begins. The counseling agency must discuss the services provided and the fees charged before starting a counseling session.

When you complete the required counseling, you must get a certificate as proof that you fulfilled the counseling requirement. You file a copy of this certificate with your bankruptcy petition. Select your counselor by going to the U.S. Trustee website, to be sure you'll be meeting with a counselor the bankruptcy court approves of. Credit-counseling agencies cannot charge extra to provide this certificate of proof.

Your best bet is to talk with your bankruptcy attorney before you set up this required counseling session. You can discuss your legal rights and hear any warnings your attorney may have about the counseling agency before your session.

In trying to pick a counselor from the U.S. Trustee list, ask these key questions by telephone before your appointment:

◆ What services do you offer?

◆ What are your fees?

◆ What if I can't afford your fees?

◆ What qualifications do your counselors have? Are they accredited or certified by an outside organization? What training do they receive?

◆ What do you do to keep information about me (including my address, phone number, and financial information) confidential and secure?

◆ How are your employees paid? Are they paid more if I sign up for certain services, if I pay a fee, or if I make a contribution to your agency?

Compare the answers you get from each of the agencies you call. Set up an appointment with the agency that you think answered your questions in the most satisfactory way. For example, if agency A says training is in-house and doesn't involve an outside certifying organization, and agency B uses outside certification, agency B likely has better-trained counselors. You can research the outside organization online. The most respected is the National Foundation for Credit Counselors (www.nfcc.org).

If employees are paid more to get you to sign up for additional services, you likely will find some pressure to do just that. So if an agency you talk with doesn't provide that incentive, you will likely experience less pressure at the meeting.

A counseling agency …

◆ Must disclose its funding sources and counselor qualifications.

◆ Must disclose the possible impact of its proposed plan on your credit report.

◆ Must disclose details about the costs of the program it recommends, if any, and how much of the costs you will pay.

◆ Must provide counseling that includes an analysis of your current financial position, how you got into that position, and how you can develop a plan to fix the problem without adding debt.

◆ Cannot use trained counselors who receive commissions or bonuses based on the outcome of the counseling.

Yet the law does appear to allow the agency to receive money from credit card companies and others for their services. That's why some people warn that you must be careful in working with credit-counseling agencies. Even though they say they are nonprofit, most receive significant funding from the credit card companies. To keep their funders (credit card companies) happy, they tend to steer people toward repayment plans even if bankruptcy may be the best choice, given a person's financial position.

If a credit-counseling agency recommends a repayment plan, it must have adequate resources to support the life of your repayment plan. For example, if the agency recommends a three-year plan, it must have adequate reserves to service your case for three years.

Debt Dangers _____

If you do have an emergency, you need to put aside your reservations and get U.S. Trustee–approved credit counseling right away. If—as has happened many, many times—your counseling session is after your case filing and the court finds no "exigent" circumstances, your bankruptcy case will either be dismissed or expunged.

Review Your Finances with Accountants

Your accountant can be a valuable resource to help you sort out your financial position, but I don't recommend that you seek out an accountant. Seek the advice of your accountant only if you've been working together for years. The amount you'll need to pay your accountant will vary greatly, and you should ask your accountant about charges before the meeting. Depending on your long-term relationship, your accountant may not even charge to review your current situation.

For example, suppose you work with an accountant because you started up a small business. Most of your debt may be consumer debt because you were unable to get business credit. That's not unusual. Few start-up small businesses can get bank loans, so people tend to use their personal credit cards to fund the business at first. If the business fails, they are stuck with a huge debt to be paid off on their credit cards.

Your accountant can advise you on your personal debt and possibly help you work out a repayment plan. After analyzing your situation, he may recommend bankruptcy as your best option. The advantage of working with your accountant is that he is paid by you and does not report to credit card companies, as do many credit counselors. You still must see a credit counselor because the bankruptcy law requires it, but you will go in with a better understanding of your financial position—and it will be harder for a credit counselor to push you toward a repayment plan if your accountant has already advised you differently.

 Credit Cleaners

You can find information about free legal help through the American Bar Association's Legal Help page (www.abanet.org/legalservices/findlegalhelp/home.cfm) or the Legal Services Corporation (www.lsc.gov), in addition to your state's bar association.

Certified Financial Planner

If you don't have an accountant but do see a certified financial planner (CFP) once or twice a year, it can't hurt to set up an appointment to review your current financial position. Your CFP will know your financial history, be able to assess the changes that got you into debt, and advise you on the best course of action.

A CFP receives more extensive training than a credit counselor. I don't recommend that you seek out a CFP if you don't already have one, but if you already work with a CFP, you can benefit from her advice before going forward with a bankruptcy.

CFP charges vary greatly, but a common hourly rate is $125. You definitely should discuss charges with your CFP before setting up a meeting. As with the accountant, you'll get professional advice about your next steps and will be better prepared to deal with the credit-counseling agency.

Talk with Debt-Relief Agencies

Under the bankruptcy law, anyone you pay or otherwise compensate to help you with your bankruptcy is considered a debt-relief agency. The two main types of debt-relief agencies are bankruptcy attorneys and bankruptcy petition preparers. Credit-counseling agencies and budget-counseling agencies are not debt-relief agencies as defined by bankruptcy law.

Before I get into the specifics of what bankruptcy attorneys and bankruptcy petition preparers do for you during the process of a bankruptcy, let's take a look at the types of contracts they can sign, the disclosures they must make, and any restrictions on their activity.

Contract

Within five days of receiving assistance from a debt-relief agency, you and the agency must enter into a contract that specifies the following:

◆ The services you will be provided

◆ The charges for those services

◆ Any terms of payment (for example, a set monthly fee for so many months)

You must get a copy of the completed, signed agreement.

Disclosures

In addition to a contract, the debt-relief agency must agree to provide services based on a series of disclosures, including these:

♦ You are required to provide your bankruptcy information in a manner that is complete, accurate, and truthful.

♦ You must completely and accurately disclose your assets and liabilities in the documents you file to start your bankruptcy case.

♦ You must research the replacement value of any asset you plan to keep and provide that value on the forms. Your attorney can assist you with this research.

♦ You must accurately provide your current monthly income and the amounts you provide in the means test. If you are filing a Chapter 13 case, you also need to provide a computation of your projected disposable income. I show you how to do that means test in Chapter 6.

♦ The information you supply could be audited; if you fail to cooperate with that audit, your bankruptcy case can be dismissed.

In addition to these warnings, the debt-relief agency must give you basic information about bankruptcy requirements and your options for help in filing and pursuing your bankruptcy case. You should get this notice within three business days of an agency first offering to provide you services. Agencies that fail to provide this information can be in big trouble. Penalties vary state-by-state because debt relief agencies are regulated by the states. Report any problems to your state attorney general.

Debt-Relief Agency Restrictions

The warnings the agency must give you are not the only things that changed with the new bankruptcy law passed in 2005. The law also introduced significant restrictions on what agencies can do.

Debt agencies …

- Must perform every service they promised to perform in the contract.

- Must counsel you to make truthful statements that are not misleading. The agency is responsible for recognizing untrue or misleading statements that seem obvious.

- Cannot counsel you to take on more debt to pay for agency services.

If the agency does not comply with these restrictions, the contract cannot be enforced against you. The debt-relief agency will be liable to you for costs and fees, including legal fees, if the agency negligently or intentionally fails to comply with provisions of the new bankruptcy law or fails to file a document, resulting in dismissal of your case or conversion to another type of bankruptcy.

These strict provisions have resulted in increased fees for filing bankruptcy. Also, many lawyers chose not to continue their bankruptcy practices because of the rigid new laws.

Legal fees for those still practicing have gone up. Polls of attorneys indicate they've raised their fees 50 percent to 100 percent since the new law passed. For a Chapter 7 filing, expect to pay between $1,500 and $3,000; for a Chapter 13 filing, expect to pay between $2,500 and $4,000. Chapter 7 fees have doubled in many cases because more documents need to be filed under the 2005 Bankruptcy Bill and the restrictions put more responsibility for accuracy on the attorney filing the case.

Bankruptcy Attorneys

Let's take a closer look at what bankruptcy attorneys do to file a bankruptcy petition. Their responsibilities differ, so let's start with Chapter 7. Most people who file for Chapter 7 bankruptcy never have to go before a judge and don't have to participate in a three- or five-year repayment plan, so that's why their legal costs are so much lower.

The primary responsibilities for a Chapter 7 bankruptcy lawyer are to be sure that all the needed paperwork is completed correctly and

accurately. The attorney also represents you at the meeting of the
creditors. Unless a lot of money is at stake and a creditor thinks he
can challenge your ability to get the debt written off, you likely will
see the bankruptcy trustee only at the meeting of the creditors.

If a mistake is made in filing the documents at the meeting of the
creditors, the case can be dismissed. So a critical responsibility of your
attorney is to be sure nothing is done wrong. Mistakes can cost you
a lot of time and money, and your case could be dismissed—meaning
your creditors could start calling again.

In some more complex Chapter 7 filings, your lawyer will not be able
to use the standard forms provided by the bankruptcy court, but will
instead need to customize the forms to your unique situation. In other
complex causes, your attorney may need to negotiate with creditors or
possibly even appear before a judge if a creditor challenges something
that the trustee cannot handle. The more complex your case is, the
higher your attorney's fees will be. I talk more about these possibili-
ties in Chapter 5.

Although you can file Chapter 7 alone if you think your case is simple
and straightforward, if you do make a mistake, your case could be dismissed. I recommend that you work with an attorney, or at least pay
for help from a bankruptcy petition preparer. I talk more about what
they do shortly.

Chapter 13 attorneys face a much more complex process that can
last as long as five years through the repayment process. Therefore,
fees are much higher, but they can be paid over time as part of your
Chapter 13 repayment plan.

Chapter 13 bankruptcy often requires a lot of negotiating with
creditors to get a repayment plan that all will agree to, and after
agreement, you and your attorney must make at least one appearance before a bankruptcy judge. If the judge confirms the plan, you're
done with the judge. Often, however, the judge will ask for changes.
You and your attorney may need to go through several confirmation
hearings until all parties agree to a repayment plan. I talk about the
variables in greater depth in Chapter 6.

Debt Dangers _____

You may find yourself negotiating with creditors and struggling to find a repayment plan acceptable to both the bankruptcy judge and your creditors. Don't try to go this route without legal representation from an attorney who is familiar with Chapter 13 procedures.

In addition to appearances before the bankruptcy trustee and judge, a Chapter 13 bankruptcy involves many variables, such as valuation of property, lien reduction, and a repayment plan that does not discriminate among debtors. Also, since life changes do happen during a three- to five-year period for most people, the attorney may have to file for plan modifications or hardship discharges if your personal financial situation changes. All this complicates your attorney's role.

Some people can't afford to pay an attorney for the full bankruptcy process, so they choose instead to pay for certain services. Consider an example. Almost everyone filing for Chapter 13 uses the stay process to protect their home. An automatic stay is placed on the home to stop all foreclosures. The lender who holds the loan may file to get that stay lifted. You may need an attorney to defend that stay even if you filed the papers for bankruptcy yourself or with the help of a bankruptcy petition preparer.

Anytime you serve as your own attorney in a bankruptcy filing, you should consider seeking the help of an attorney for specific services if it means defending your ability to keep a certain asset or discharge a certain debt of considerable value to you. For example, suppose you owe $12,000 on a credit card and the creditor is refusing to accept your payment plan. You may want to hire an attorney to negotiate with that creditor because the attorney's fee may save you a lot of money in the long term on the repayment plan.

If your filing is complex and you need to hire an attorney to do more than what is specified in the original contract agreement, you can expect to be charged $200 to $300 per hour for additional work needed. Attorneys also charge between $400 and $600 for additional court appearances.

Most bankruptcy attorneys will meet with you for a free consultation before taking the case. During this consultation, they'll review your financial position and make a recommendation about how you should proceed. They should also lay out what their costs would be to represent you in a bankruptcy based on the type of bankruptcy they recommend.

Bankruptcy Petition Preparers

Let's take a closer look at what bankruptcy petition preparers can do for you. Essentially, they will help you prepare your forms for filing your bankruptcy petition. This includes helping you organize the information in the way the court expects, as well as typing the forms.

Bankruptcy petition preparers are not lawyers, but they are familiar with the bankruptcy courts in your area. Their primary responsibility is to use the information you provide about your debts, property, income, expenses, and economic transactions during the previous year or two. The bankruptcy law prohibits them from giving legal advice.

They cannot give advice in these areas:

◆ The type of bankruptcy you should file

◆ What debts will be discharged

◆ Whether you can save your home

◆ Tax consequences of debt discharge

◆ Whether you should repay or agree to reaffirm a debt

◆ Bankruptcy procedures and rights

The primary responsibilities of bankruptcy petition preparers are to give you some information about basic bankruptcy tasks, such as how to deal with secured debts and choose exemptions. But you will have to make your own decisions about how to proceed.

You should expect a fee of between $200 and $250 to have your petition papers prepared by a bankruptcy petition preparer. Bankruptcy petition preparers must submit a statement under oath with each petition stating what you paid to them in the previous 12 months and any fees that you might still owe them. If the court rules that you were charged more than allowed, the preparer will have to repay you.

If the court finds that the preparer engaged in a fraudulent act or failed to comply with the rules governing his actions, he could be required to return your entire fee.

What If You Can't Afford to Pay an Attorney?

You may find that you cannot afford to pay an attorney. Some states have legal aid offices that will help with bankruptcy filings. Call your local legal aid office to see if you can get some help filing for bankruptcy. You must be in a low income bracket to get help from legal aid.

If you're located near a law school, many law schools have legal clinics that provide free legal advice to consumers. You will be aided primarily by a law student, but one of the law school professors will review the work, so that's better than trying to file bankruptcy on your own. To get help, you must show that you are in a low to moderate income bracket.

Now that we've met the key professionals who may assist you with your bankruptcy decisions and filing, let's take a closer look at the basics of filing for bankruptcy.

The Least You Need to Know

- ◆ You must see a credit counselor approved by the bankruptcy court before filing for bankruptcy.

- ◆ Bankruptcy attorneys assist you in the process of bankruptcy, but they do have a responsibility to recognize obvious lies and misstatements.

- ◆ You can file for bankruptcy without an attorney, but for certain proceedings, you may want to hire an attorney to help with your defense.

- ◆ If you can't afford an attorney, you may be able to find free legal assistance from your state's legal aid or from a law school's legal clinic.

Part 2

Understanding the Bankruptcy Process

In this part, I help you understand what you need to know before filing for bankruptcy. After that, I dive deeply into the details of how you actually file for Chapter 7 and Chapter 13 bankruptcies. Finally, I cover the key issues to consider when picking the bankruptcy that is right for you.

Chapter 4

Filing for Bankruptcy

In This Chapter

- ◆ Monthly income
- ◆ Do-it-yourself versus get help
- ◆ The impact of filing
- ◆ The bankruptcy court

You've considered the alternatives to bankruptcy. You've decided that personal bankruptcy is the right way for you to get back on track financially.

You're now ready to find out the type of bankruptcy you qualify for—and get started. I discuss how your income plays a key role in the type of bankruptcy you must consider, and then take a closer look at what constitutes income. I briefly discuss whether to file for bankruptcy on your own or with an attorney. Then I review what happens when you first file for bankruptcy. I look at the way to determine which of your assets will become part of your bankruptcy estate. And I take a quick look at working with the bankruptcy court.

Are You Eligible?

Eligibility for bankruptcy depends on two key factors: your income and the source of your debts. For both Chapter 7 and Chapter 13 bankruptcies, your outstanding debt must be primarily consumer debt. If most of the debt you owe is related to a business, you must file Chapter 11 bankruptcy. If your debt is related to family farming or fishing, you must file Chapter 12 bankruptcy.

To qualify for Chapter 7 bankruptcy, your income must be below the median income for your state. That median income varies by the state you live in and by the number of people in your family.

Credit Cleaners

You can check the median income for your state at the Census Bureau website (www. census.gov/hhes/www/ income/statemedfaminc.html).

If you earn more than the median income for your state, you must take a means test, which looks at your sources of income and your expenses. I show you how to take that means test in Chapter 5.

Chapter 13 is the catch-all for most other people filing with consumer debt. If your secured debts exceed $1,010,650 or your unsecured debt exceeds $336,900—inflation adjustments may be made periodically to these amounts—you must file for Chapter 11 bankruptcy.

Chapter 13 has a different kind of means test than Chapter 7. This test looks at how much income you have and whether you will need to develop a plan to repay at least some of your debt in three years or five years. I show you how to take that test and examine what it means in Chapter 6.

Your Official Income

Before you can even think of filing, you must determine your current monthly income and whether you'll have any money left after expenses to repay your creditors.

Bankruptcy law defines current monthly income as the average monthly income you received during the six-month period that ended the last day of the month before you file for bankruptcy. The monthly income is calculated based on your gross salary, not on the net paycheck you receive after taxes and benefit deductions have been taken out.

When you calculate your income, you must include all sources of income except these three types:

♦ Payments you get under the Social Security Act, including Social Security retirement, Supplemental Security income (SSI), and Social Security Disability (SSDI)

♦ Payments to victims of war crimes or crimes against humanity, based on your status as a victim of such crimes

♦ Payments to victims of international or domestic terrorism

You must include these income sources in the calculation:

♦ Wages, salary, tips, bonuses, overtime, and commissions.

♦ Net income from the operation of a business or profession. Essentially, this is the amount you would report as net income on a *Schedule C* tax form, subtracting reasonable and necessary business expenses from your gross business income.

def•i•ni•tion

> **Schedule C** is a form attached to your individual income tax Form 1040 to report the profit and loss from a business.

♦ Interest, dividends, and royalties.

♦ Net income from rents and other real property income.

♦ Pension and retirement income.

♦ Regular contributions to the household expenses from your children or spouse.

♦ Regular contributions from your spouse if he or she isn't a joint debtor in the bankruptcy.

- ◆ Unemployment compensation.
- ◆ Workers' compensation insurance.
- ◆ State disability insurance.
- ◆ Annuity payments.

Let's take a look at what happens to Joe, Mary, and their two children who live in Arkansas. Joe and Mary's bills are mounting, and they just can't pay off all their creditors. They are exploring filing for Chapter 7 bankruptcy.

Joe lost his job, which paid $5,000 per month. With unemployment insurance, Joe gets $1,200 per month. While Joe is unemployed, Mary finds a part-time job for which she is paid $2,000 per month. If they file for joint bankruptcy after just three months of unemployment for Joe, the six-month calculation will have to include three months at $5,000 and three months at $3,200. So here's how to calculate their six-month average:

1. Multiply $5,000 by 3 = $15,000

2. Multiply $3,200 by 3 = $ 9,600

3. Total these calculations to find the total income earned for 6 months—$24,600

4. Find the average monthly income by dividing the total income ($24,600) by 6 months = $4,100

def•i•ni•tion

Median income means that the dollar figure for salary is exactly in the middle of income earners. The same number of people earn less than the median as those who earn more.

So the couple's average monthly income would be $4,100. Now that we've completed that calculation, we must compare it to the *median income* for their state. You can find the median for your state by going to the website of the U.S. Census Bureau (www.census.gov/hhes/www/income/statemedfaminc.html). The bankruptcy court uses Census

Bureau data to determine median income by family size. Remember, your gross household income must be below the median income to qualify for Chapter 7 bankruptcy.

In looking at the median income chart, the median incomes for the state of Arkansas in 2008 (the most recent data available) show that a family of two has a median income of $41,760. If Joe and Mary have two children, they can earn as much as $53,671 and still fall below the median income level, which means they qualify for Chapter 7 bankruptcy. If they have more than two children, they can add another $6,900 per family member to the $53,671 to determine the allowable median income to file for Chapter 7 bankruptcy.

So do Joe and Mary match the median income for the Arkansas? Multiply $4,100, their monthly income, by 12, which totals $49,200. They fall well within the limits for a family of four.

Credit Cleaners

Since the bankruptcy court looks back six months, if you've recently lost a job, you may find that if you're able to hold off by one or two months after your termination date before filing for bankruptcy, you'll meet the requirements for Chapter 7 bankruptcy. If not, your income may be too high to file for Chapter 7 bankruptcy and you'll have to repay at least some debt.

Filing on Your Own vs. with Legal Help

Although you could file for bankruptcy on your own, I highly recommend that you don't use the do-it-yourself approach. As you read through the requirements for filing each type of bankruptcy and review the discussion about passing the means test or developing a repayment plan, determining what to include as assets in your bankruptcy estate, listing all your debts appropriately, and filing the correct paperwork, you'll find this entire process very overwhelming. You can find it even more overwhelming if you're facing a foreclosure on your home.

Another key factor is that if you make a mistake, your bankruptcy case could get dismissed and you'll be back to square one. You won't be able to even file again for six months. You'll be back to dealing with harassing creditors.

In a worst-case scenario, you might not have correctly understood the homestead exemption and exceptions rules (see Appendix C) for your state. Once you file, your finances are in the hands of the bankruptcy trustee. If he determines that he must sell your house to satisfy creditors, you might not want to agree to that. If you've filed for Chapter 7, though, you may have no choice.

Although the bankruptcy trustee will assist you to be certain you've filed the papers correctly, you must remember that his primary responsibility is to the creditors and making sure that they get their fair share of whatever you have left in your bankruptcy estate.

Debt Dangers

What is really treacherous about Chapter 7 is that—unlike Chapter 13—you cannot just choose to dismiss your case, no questions asked. Your motion to dismiss a Chapter 7 must be heard by the judge, and the trustee may well oppose dismissal.

A competent attorney that you pay will be looking out for your best interests. If you can't afford an attorney, you may qualify for free legal services. Contact your state or local bar association for information about legal help. Many law schools also have legal clinics that offer free legal services. Yes, you'll be working with a law student, but that law student can go to a professor for help with any difficult issues.

If you do want to do it yourself, look for basic information on the website for the bankruptcy court where you will be filing (see www.uscourts.gov/courtlinks). You can find bankruptcy resources at the U.S. Court's website (www.uscourts.gov/bankruptcycourts/resources.html), including all the forms you will need and detailed information about bankruptcy basics.

Immediate Impact of Filing

When you file for bankruptcy, most debt collectors can't call you. They must work with the bankruptcy court. If you do get a call from a debt collector, tell them you filed bankruptcy and to deal with the bankruptcy court. Foreclosures on your home are stopped, too, though you or your attorney would need to be sure to get the bankruptcy docket number to the foreclosing attorney.

Creditors and Collections

After filing for bankruptcy, an "automatic stay" goes into effect. This prohibits creditors and collection agencies from continuing their collection activities unless they get special permission from the bankruptcy court to continue collecting. If the creditor wants to have the stay lifted, he can file a motion called "Motion to Lift Stay."

Most creditors are stopped dead in their tracks and won't get the stay lifted. They must stop all harassing calls, threatening letters from lawyers, and lawsuits seeking money judgments for credit card and health-care bills. They cannot try to collect attorney fees, debts arising from breach of contract, or most legal judgments against you.

The IRS can continue certain actions after you file bankruptcy. It can continue a tax audit, issue a tax deficiency notice, demand a tax return, issue a tax assessment, and demand payment of a tax assessment. The bankruptcy filing does stop the IRS from issuing a lien against your property or seizing your property or income.

The automatic stay stops creditors from …

- Filing a lawsuit or proceeding with a pending lawsuit.
- Recording a lien against your property.
- Reporting debt to a credit-reporting bureau.
- Seizing your property or income, such as garnishing a paycheck or seizing money in your bank account.

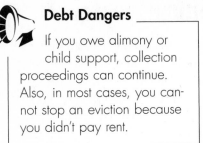

Debt Dangers

If you owe alimony or child support, collection proceedings can continue. Also, in most cases, you cannot stop an eviction because you didn't pay rent.

Utility companies cannot discontinue service because you filed for bankruptcy, but they can shut off your service 20 days after you file if you don't provide them with a deposit or other means to assure future payment. They can also shut off service if you don't pay for services you received after filing for bankruptcy.

Criminal proceedings against you can continue for the nondebt components of the case, but any aspect of the case related to debt cannot continue until after the bankruptcy court makes a determination.

Foreclosures

The automatic stay you get from filing for bankruptcy will stop a foreclosure. But if you filed another bankruptcy within the previous two years and the bankruptcy court in the earlier proceeding lifted the stay, you can't reinstate the stay by filing another bankruptcy.

If you had a second bankruptcy case pending during the previous year, the stay will terminate as to the debtor after 30 days unless you, the bankruptcy trustee, or the creditor asks for the stay to continue. You must prove that the current case was filed in good faith. Some people file a bankruptcy and then withdraw it or the case is dismissed because a person should have filed under Chapter 13 instead of Chapter 7. Even though the 2005 law made it possible for the stay to be lifted, the bankruptcy courts in most cases allow you to keep protection even if you had a second case pending within a year. If you are filing bankruptcy for the second time in a 12-month period, be sure to discuss this with your attorney.

If you had more than two bankruptcy cases pending during the previous year, though, then your attorney will have to file a motion to impose the automatic stay, protecting your home and other property.

Determine Assets in Your Bankruptcy Estate

Any property you own on the day you file for bankruptcy is part of the bankruptcy estate. In most Chapter 7 cases, property you buy and income you acquire after you file for bankruptcy are not included in the estate. When you do file for bankruptcy, you must complete three forms: one lists personal property, one lists real estate property, and one lists property you claim as exempt.

So what exactly is in your bankruptcy estate?

◆ Property in your possession that you own

◆ Property not in your possession that you own

◆ Property you are entitled to receive in the future

Let's take a closer look at what falls into each category. We'll also look at marital property and what happens to it.

Property in Your Possession That You Own

This includes everything you own, whether or not you owe money on the item: your car, real estate holdings, clothing, books, furniture, tools, boat, artwork, television, fishing gear or gear related to other hobbies, golf clubs, and anything else you own.

 Debt Dangers

You can sometimes forget about a possession, such as the rights to a family plot of land, when you file for bankruptcy. For example, if your name is listed as one of the owners on a plot of land or a family business, your share in that property will become part of the bankruptcy estate. So if your family does own property and you think your name might be on it, be sure to check that out before filing. Your family could be forced to sell the property to raise cash to cover your debt, based on your share of the ownership.

If you have property in your possession that belongs to someone else, such as a car you borrowed from a friend, it does not become part of your bankruptcy estate. You can't be forced to sell something you don't own to raise money to pay your creditors.

Property Not in Your Possession That You Own

Even if someone else has possession of property you own at the time of filing, it will be considered part of your bankruptcy estate. A common example of assets not in one's possession are stock certificates held by your broker, security deposits held by your utility companies or your landlord, or assets you have because of money you invested in a business. All of these items become part of your bankruptcy estate.

Property You Are Entitled to Receive in the Future

Any property that you have a legal right to receive but have not yet gotten is included in your bankruptcy estate. This can include the following:

- ◆ Wages, royalties, or commissions you have earned but not yet received
- ◆ A tax refund due to you
- ◆ Vacation pay or severance pay you're expected to get
- ◆ Property you inherited after the death of someone
- ◆ A settlement or insurance payment due based on a death or injury that occurred
- ◆ Any money due to you in payment for goods or services you provided

You can't file for bankruptcy before a large severance check or insurance payment comes in and leave it out of the bankruptcy. If a large payment, such as an insurance payment for death benefits, comes due after you've filed for bankruptcy, it likely will not become part of the bankruptcy estate.

Marital Property and Bankruptcy

If you are married, how property is handled in a bankruptcy differs based on whether you live in a community property or common-law property state. Community property states include Arizona, California, Idaho, Louisiana, Nevada, New Mexico, Texas, Washington, and Wisconsin. In Alaska, you can write in community property agreements as part of a marital estate or trust.

If you file jointly for bankruptcy in a community property state, all your property is included in the bankruptcy estate. Some gifts and inheritances can be held as the separate property of one of the spouses. If you don't have any separate property, all the community property becomes part of the bankruptcy estate, even if only one spouse files the bankruptcy. So if you're in a community property state, don't expect to keep much out of the bankruptcy estate by filing separately.

All states not mentioned previously are common-law property states. If you file for bankruptcy jointly in a common-law state, all the property you own jointly and separately becomes part of the bankruptcy estate. But if only one spouse files for bankruptcy, the bankruptcy estate includes that spouse's separate property (property only in the spouse's name) and half of the property that is jointly owned.

Some states have different rules for property owned as *tenancy by the entirety*. If you live in Delaware, the District of Columbia, Florida, Hawaii, Illinois, Indiana, Maryland, Massachusetts, Michigan, Missouri, North Carolina, Pennsylvania, Tennessee, Vermont, Virginia, or Wyoming and you own property using tenancy by the entirety, you have additional protection when you

def•i•ni•tion

Tenancy by the entirety is a way couples can hold property in about half the states. When one spouse dies, the surviving spouse automatically owns 100 percent of the property. In most cases, this type of property is not part of the bankruptcy estate if only one person files.

file for bankruptcy. If only one spouse files for bankruptcy, creditors or the bankruptcy court cannot take property that is owned jointly. If you live in a state with this provision, be sure to talk with your bankruptcy attorney about how to take advantage of it if you plan to file for bankruptcy.

Working With the Bankruptcy Court

After you file for bankruptcy, your financial assets, as well as your financial problems, fall into the hands of the bankruptcy trustee. Most of your contact—or your attorney's—with the bankruptcy court will be with the trustee or his staff.

When you file, the bankruptcy trustee assumes legal control of your property and debts. You can't sell or give away property while your case is open; if you do, the bankruptcy trustee can ask that your case be dismissed.

The bankruptcy trustee has two key duties:

- Making sure that your unsecured creditors are paid as much as possible on the debts you owe them
- Making sure that you comply with the bankruptcy laws

In many cases, the bankruptcy trustee is either a local bankruptcy lawyer or a nonlawyer who is very knowledgeable about Chapter 7 or Chapter 13 bankruptcies and the local court rules and procedures. The rules differ in each state because the amount of property that you can exempt from the bankruptcy differs depending on state law. This is particularly significant when it comes to saving your property. In Appendix C, we detail these state differences.

When the court receives your bankruptcy filing, it sends you a Notice of Filing that gives you the name, business address, and business phone number for the bankruptcy trustee assigned to you. In very rare cases, the trustee will then follow up with a list of any financial documents he wants to see, such as bank statements, property appraisals, or canceled checks. He'll give you a deadline for producing this information.

In addition to the bankruptcy trustee, a U.S. Trustee will be involved, but you probably won't meet him. The Office of U.S. Trustee is part of the United States Department of Justice. This trustee supervises the trustees who actually handle the cases with debtors. The U.S. Trustee monitors cases to be sure that the bankruptcy laws are being followed and that any question of fraud or criminal activity is appropriately handled. There are 21 regional U.S. Trustee offices throughout the country.

You definitely want to avoid their direct participation in your bankruptcy filing because it will be a sign of trouble. When might the U.S. Trustee get involved? Here are some common problems that arise:

- A person's reported current monthly income is proved to be more than the median income for your state during testimony at the creditor's meeting.

- You earn enough income to support a Chapter 13 repayment plan even though you filed for Chapter 7.

- You engaged in illegal actions that warrant a fraud investigation, such as lying on your bankruptcy paperwork.

- Your case is picked for a random audit. About 250 bankruptcy cases are audited each year according to the rules under the bankruptcy law.

Now that you know the basics of what goes into a bankruptcy filing, let's take a closer look at how to file for Chapter 7.

The Least You Need to Know

- You must earn less than your state's median income to file for Chapter 7 bankruptcy or face a means test.

- Although you can file for bankruptcy without an attorney, to best protect your interests, you should seek legal counsel.

- Filing for bankruptcy can stop creditors from calling and can halt a foreclosure on your home.

- You must carefully list everything you own as part of the bankruptcy estate, whether it's in your possession or not.

Chapter 5

Chapter 7 Bankruptcy Process

In This Chapter

- ◆ Income eligibility tests
- ◆ Filing and its costs
- ◆ Property—safe and at risk
- ◆ The role of creditors and the bankruptcy trustee
- ◆ Erasing debt

You've decided that you'd like to wipe out all your unsecured debt and get a fresh start. If you're not worried about losing assets, Chapter 7 is the best way to do that, but you must be sure you qualify to file for Chapter 7 bankruptcy.

In this chapter, I show you how to test your income for qualification. Then I talk about the filing fees, take a look at what happens to your property, discuss what to expect when you meet your creditors, and review the duties of the bankruptcy trustee and judge in a Chapter 7 filing. I also discuss how a Chapter 7 bankruptcy filing ends.

What Is Chapter 7?

Chapter 7 bankruptcy is the type of bankruptcy in which you can *liquidate* all your debts. You don't have to pay back any of the debt discharged by the bankruptcy court at the end of the bankruptcy.

def•i•ni•tion _____

> **Liquidate** means to pay down all your debt. Some of your property may need to be sold to pay down that debt.

But since your debt is being liquidated, some of your property may have to be sold to satisfy that debt.

The Counseling Requirement

So how do you get started? If you haven't already met with a credit counselor, as discussed in Chapter 3, you must do so before you file for Chapter 7 bankruptcy. The fee for this counseling is typically no more than $50, but it can be waived if you discuss that waiver with the counselor before the counseling session.

If you have to file for bankruptcy immediately to stop garnishment of your wages, prevent a foreclosure on your home, or stop the IRS from seizing property, but you can't get an appointment with a counselor within five days of requesting one, you can file for bankruptcy before meeting with a credit counselor. However, you must prove that you've seen a credit counselor within 30 days of filing for bankruptcy. You can ask the bankruptcy court to extend this deadline another 15 days.

You also may be able to avoid the credit counseling requirement, but you'll have to notify the bankruptcy court of why you want a waiver and you must attend a hearing. Here are reasons to ask for a waiver of credit counseling:

◆ You have a physical disability that prevents you from attending counseling. Since you can be counseled by telephone and over the Internet, this likely won't be successful for most disabilities.

◆ You are mentally incapacitated and cannot understand and benefit from counseling.

◆ You are on active duty in a military combat zone.

Median Income and the Means Test

Next you need to calculate your income. I talk about how to do that in Chapter 4. You then need to determine whether you are below the median income for the state in which you live. You are eligible to file for Chapter 7 bankruptcy as long as your debts are primarily consumer debts and not business debts.

If your gross household income is above your state's median income, you must complete the second part of the means test as part of your filing. Do this test first before you fill out any of the other bankruptcy paperwork. If you don't pass the means test, you'll have to file under Chapter 13, with a term of five years. Disabled veterans also can skip the means test.

The primary purpose of the means test is to find out whether you have enough disposable income left after allowable expenses to pay back some of your debt. If you do, you will have to file for Chapter 13 bankruptcy instead of Chapter 7 bankruptcy.

 Credit Cleaners

Most filers are finding that they don't have to take a means test. Surveys have shown that only about 15 percent of filers take a means test.

The means test requires you to …

♦ Calculate your total monthly income.

♦ Subtract allowable IRS expense amounts.

♦ Subtract secured and priority debt payments to see what you would have left over each month.

♦ Find out whether you have enough left to pay other debts.

If you have at least $110 a month left over and can pay more than 25 percent of your unsecured, nonpriority debts over a five-year period, you'll likely have to file for Chapter 13 bankruptcy. Let's take a closer look at each of these steps.

Step 1—Calculate Your Total Monthly Income

I showed you how to calculate your monthly income in Chapter 4, so refer back to that chapter if you need a refresher.

Step 2—Subtract Allowable IRS Expense Amounts

You're allowed to subtract certain expenses based on standards developed by the IRS:

◆ **Food, clothing, and other items**—You can get the IRS allowable costs at www.irs.gov/businesses/small/article/ 0,,id=104627,00.html. At the time this book was written, the total costs for this category ranged from $517 for one person to $1,370 for four people. If your household includes more than four people, the IRS standards permit you to add $262.

◆ **Housing**—The IRS housing standards are calculated by the county in which you live. You can find the IRS standards at www.irs.gov/businesses/small/article/0,,id=104696,00.html.

◆ **Transportation**—The IRS divides transportation into two categories: general transportation (includes car maintenance or public transportation) and transportation ownership expenses (includes car loans or leases). For calculating allowable monthly expenses, you should use the numbers for general transportation at www.irs.gov/businesses/small/article/0,,id=104623,00.html. The national public transportation rate was $173 at the time of this writing, but operation of cars varied by region.

In addition to these IRS standards, you can subtract the following:

◆ **Charitable contributions**—Total the monthly amount you donate to charity.

◆ **Child care**—Total the average monthly amount you spend on child care. Don't include payments for primary and secondary education in this calculation.

- **Communication**—Total the average monthly amount you spend on cellphones, pagers, call waiting, caller identification, and special long-distance or Internet services that are necessary for the welfare of you or your family.

- **Court-ordered payments**—Total the amount you pay monthly pursuant to a court order, such as spousal support and child support payments.

- **Dependent care**—Total the reasonable expenses needed to care for an elderly, chronically ill, or disabled family member.

- **Domestic violence**—Total the reasonable expenses to maintain your safety and the safety of your family.

- **Education**—You can add up to $1,650 per year per child for public or private elementary or secondary school, if you can show that it's a reasonable expense and is not covered by the IRS guidelines.

- **Health care**—Total the average monthly amount that you actually pay for health-care expenses that are not reimbursed by your health insurance or paid by a health savings account.

- **Insurance**—Total your average monthly premiums for term life, dental, vision, long-term care, and any other insurance payments that were not included in other places, such as payroll deductions.

- **Mandatory payroll deductions**—Total the average monthly amount that is taken out of your paycheck. This can include mandatory retirement contributions, union dues, and uniform costs. You can't include discretionary amounts, such as voluntary 401(k) contributions.

- **Taxes**—Total the average monthly amount you incur for federal, state, and local taxes. This can include income taxes, self-employment taxes, Social Security taxes, and Medicare taxes. Don't include any real estate or sales taxes.

Total the amount of these allowable expenses to find out your average allowable monthly expenses.

Now you're ready to calculate your net monthly income:

Total average monthly income   _____

Minus allowable monthly expenses   (_____)

Net monthly income after allowable expenses   _____

If your net monthly income is less than $110, you've passed the means test and you don't need to go any further. If your net monthly income is above $110, go on to Step 3. When filing, you can use a worksheet to show this allowable monthly expense calculation.

Debt Dangers _____

> Don't try to fudge your numbers to get the net monthly income under $110. If the bankruptcy trustee determines that you didn't calculate your numbers for the means test accurately, he can dismiss the case or force you to file under Chapter 13 and repay part of the debt.

Step 3—Subtract Secured and Priority Debt Payments

If your net monthly income is more than $110, you need to calculate your monthly disposable income. This calculation determines how much money you have left over each month after you pay your mandatory debts. These mandatory debts include your secured and priority debts.

First, calculate a monthly payment for secured debts:

- Total due in payments for the next five years on your mortgage
- Total due over the next five years on your car note
- Total due over the next five months on any other debts secured by property, such as an equity line, a lien, or a personal loan

Now total all your secured payments you owe over the next five years and divide that by 60 to determine how much you would have to pay on these debts each month for the next five years. The calculation would be as follows:

Total mortgage payments	$_____
Total car note payments	$_____
Total other secured debt payments	$_____
Total secured debt payments for five years	$_____
Total secured debt – _____/60 =	$_____

These are your monthly secured payments.

Next, calculate a monthly payment for arrearages (amounts past due):

♦ Total arrearage on your mortgage and equity or second mortgage

♦ Total arrearage on your car loan

♦ Total arrearage on any other secured debt

Now total all arrearages and divide that number by 60 to get a monthly amount you would need to pay off all your arrearages.

Total mortgage arrearages	$_____
Total car loan arrearages	$_____
Total other secured debt arrearages	$_____
Total arrearages for five years	$_____
Total arrearages – _____/60 =	$_____

These are your monthly payments for arrearages.

Now calculate your priority debts:

♦ Total how much you owe for back child support and alimony

♦ Total how much you owe in back income taxes

♦ Total how much you owe on all other priority debts, which can include secured credit cards, personal loans secured by your home or other assets, and liens against your property

Total all your priority debts and divide that number by 60 to determine how much you would need each month to pay off your priority debts.

> Total child support payments $\qquad$ $_____
>
> Total back income taxes $\qquad$ $_____
>
> Total other priority payments $\qquad$ $_____
>
> Total priority payments for five years $\qquad$ $_____
>
> Total priority debt _____/60 = $\qquad$ $_____

This is your monthly payments for your priority debts.

Next, calculate your total for your monthly secured and priority debts:

> Total of your monthly payments to secured debts $\qquad$ $_____
>
> Total of your monthly payments to arrearages $\qquad$ $_____
>
> Total of your monthly payments to priority debts $\qquad$ $_____
>
> Total for monthly secured and priority debts $\qquad$ $_____

Now you need to calculate your monthly disposable income. Start with the number you calculated in Step 2—net income after allowable expenses. As I said earlier, you need to do this step only if your net income is above $110.

> Net income after allowable expenses $\qquad$ $_____
>
> Subtract your total for monthly and
> secured priority debts $\qquad$ ($_____)
>
> Amount left over to pay unsecured debts $\qquad$ $_____

Finally, you must calculate your monthly disposable income. You do this by multiplying the amount of money left over to pay unsecured debts by the administrative expenses multiplier for your judicial district. For example, in the Middle and South Districts of Florida, the multiplier was 8.8 percent at the time of this writing; in northern Florida, the multiplier was 10 percent. The administrative expenses primarily relate to the amount it would cost to pay the bankruptcy trustee for administering the bankruptcy payoff if you were to file for a Chapter 13 bankruptcy. I talk more about these fees and how they work in Chapter 6.

Credit Cleaners _____

You can find the administrative expenses multiplier for your district at www.usdoj.gov/ust/eo/bapcpa/20090315/bci_data/ch13_exp_mult.htm. Bankruptcy court districts set these multipliers.

To calculate your monthly disposable income, do this:

Amount left over to pay unsecured debts $_____

Subtract calculation for the
administrative expenses   ($_____)

Equals monthly disposable income $_____

If your monthly disposable income is less than $110 per month, you've passed the means test and can skip Step 4. You are eligible for filing for Chapter 7 bankruptcy, provided that you meet the other eligibility requirements.

But if your monthly disposable income is more than $110, you still have one step to go to see if you can pass the means test. If you don't, your only option will be to file for Chapter 13 and set up a repayment plan. You will not be able to ask that all your debts be discharged.

Step 4—Find Out What's Left to Pay Other Debts

This is the final step in determining whether you can file for Chapter 7 bankruptcy or will be limited to filing under Chapter 13. In this case, the bankruptcy court is testing whether you can pay at least $10,950 toward your unsecured, nonpriority debt over a five-year period or pay one quarter of your debt.

First, multiply your monthly disposable income (calculated in Step 3) by 60. This gives you your monthly disposable income for the next five years.

Monthly disposable income $_____ × 60 = $_____

This is your disposable income for five years. You will need this number as we calculate your income available to pay off debt.

Next, add up your unsecured, nonpriority debts:

- Alimony and child support
- Back rent
- Church or synagogue dues
- Credit and charge card purchases
- Deficiency judgments from secured loans
- Department store credit card purchases
- Health club dues
- Lawyer and accountant bills
- Loans from friends or relatives
- Medical bills
- Money judgments from contract disputes
- Money judgments from negligent behavior
- Student loans
- Union dues
- Utility bills
- Other debts

Now you need to total these unsecured debts. Multiply that number by 25 percent. If your answer is less than your total monthly disposable income for the next five years, which you calculated earlier, you have passed the means test and you don't need to continue.

Total unsecured debts $_____ × 25% = $_____

Compare this number to the total monthly disposable income. If the total of 25 percent of your unsecured debts is less than your total, you've passed the means test.

If your total monthly disposable income is equal to or larger than 25 percent of your total unsecured debts, you've failed the means test unless you can prove special circumstances. You likely will need to file for Chapter 13 bankruptcy, but do verify your calculations with an attorney to be sure you've interpreted everything correctly.

Debt Dangers

If you file for Chapter 7 bankruptcy and make a mistake when calculating your means test, one of two things can happen. If you fail the means test, your case can be dismissed or the bankruptcy trustee can convert your case to a Chapter 13 case.

You have one more chance to try to file as a Chapter 7 bankruptcy case if you can prove special circumstances. The 2005 bankruptcy law does not define the term *special circumstances*, but Congress cited a "serious medical condition" or "a call or order to active duty in the Armed Forces" as two examples of special circumstances. Check with your attorney if you think your situation may qualify for special circumstances.

Please do not despair at the superhuman intellect needed to parse the requirements of the means test. Almost any attorney you consult will have bankruptcy software that magically produces green or red lights within the means test tab. With relatively little effort, your attorney can look for the one green light or, worse, for the two red lights and tell you where you stand.

Bottom line here is that if your gross household income is well below your state's median income and if your unsecured assets are minimal, you may conceivably be able to proceed without an attorney. If your gross household income is close to or above your state's median income, go ahead, splurge, and hire an attorney.

More Eligibility Requirements

If you do pass the means tests, you must consider a few other eligibility requirements before you file.

- You must be an individual, a married couple, or a sole proprietor with a small business who has personal responsibility for the business debts. You can include these business debts, even if they are a majority of the debt outstanding.

- You haven't had a previous Chapter 7 bankruptcy discharge filed within the last eight years or a Chapter 13 discharge within the last six years.

- You previously filed a bankruptcy that was dismissed. It must be at least 180 days since that filing, if your previous bankruptcy filing was dismissed because you violated a court order, the court ruled your filing was fraudulent or that it was abusive use of the bankruptcy system, or you requested a dismissal after a creditor asked the court to lift an automatic stay.

- You can prove that you have not been dishonest with your debtors. For example, concealing assets by giving them to friends and families is a big no-no. You can also get in trouble if you run up large debts for luxury items and have no way to pay for them.

As long as you pass the means test and meet the eligibility requirements, you're ready to file for Chapter 7 bankruptcy. Whether this is the right option for you depends on your circumstances. In Chapter 7, I compare bankruptcy options and examine how your choice could impact your assets and your life after bankruptcy.

Filing

If you believe you pass the means test and meet the other eligibility requirements, you're ready to file for bankruptcy. The actual act of filing is filling out your bankruptcy petition, which is a packet of forms you can find at the bankruptcy courts web page.

Credit Cleaners

You can find all the forms you need to file for bankruptcy at www.
uscourts.gov/bkforms/bankruptcy_forms.html. But even if you don't
want to hire an attorney to help you file for bankruptcy, I recommend that you hire a bankruptcy petition preparer to help you figure out
which forms to use and how to fill them out appropriately.

Filing for a Chapter 7 bankruptcy costs $299. If you can't afford the
fee, you can file for a waiver or for permission to pay the fee in installments. If you want a lawyer to represent you, you'll likely pay between
$1,500 and $2,000. If you decide to file on your own but hire a bankruptcy petition preparer, the cost will be between $150 and $200.

After you file, your bankruptcy trustee will be chosen randomly from
a panel, which is usually made up of lawyers but can also include lay-
people familiar with bankruptcy and state law. You'll get a letter from
the trustee about two weeks after you file, with a date set for your
"341 meeting," also known as the meeting of your creditors.

In addition to sending you a letter, your bankruptcy trustee will
notify all the creditors you listed on your bankruptcy forms. Once
creditors receive their letters, they no longer can contact you directly;
they must work with the bankruptcy court. Your creditors will get a
notice that says your case at present shows no nonexempt assets for
distribution. They will also be told there is no need to file a "proof of
claim" with the bankruptcy court.

Credit Cleaners

If you do get a call from a creditor after you've filed bankruptcy,
tell them that you've filed bankruptcy and that they must contact the
bankruptcy court. By law, they can no longer harass you.

Working With the Bankruptcy Trustee

Your bankruptcy trustee's primary responsibility is to sell property
you own and dole out the proceeds to creditors. Any assets that do not

fall under the protections offered by your state's homestead exemption (see Appendix C) can be sold to satisfy your debts. The trustee also can take any money that you received within six months of filing for bankruptcy, such as life insurance benefits, inheritances, or divorce property divisions, to satisfy your debtors.

In addition to selling property, the trustee could recover some of the transfers you made before filing:

- **Fraudulent transfers**—You may decide to give valuable property to friends or relatives so your creditors won't get it. That's a fraudulent transfer. Anything you give away in the 12 months before you file bankruptcy can be considered fraudulent. If you conceal these transfers from a bankruptcy trustee, you may go to jail. At the very least, your debt discharge will be denied. The trustee can also go after the recipient of a fraudulent transfer.

- **Preferential transfers**—These are transfers you made to pay a debt to a specific creditor just before filing bankruptcy. For example, suppose that you decided to file for bankruptcy but wanted to be sure your family doctor was paid in full. The bankruptcy trustee can get that money back from your family doctor. The bankruptcy trustee can look back at your payments made 90 days before filing for bankruptcy.

- **Unperfected liens**—To be perfected, liens must be filed with the clerk of the court. For example, if a mortgager neglects to file a lien against your property after you agree to a mortgage, that's an unperfected lien. As another example, when a creditor wins a judgment in court, the creditor must file that lien against your property with the local clerk of the court. If the lien is not filed with the clerk of the court before you file for bankruptcy, it is an unperfected lien. Then the creditor, who thought he had a secured debt, will have to wait in line with the unsecured creditors.

The bankruptcy trustee makes his money on commission based on what he can recover for your creditors. He won't go scrounging through your belongings to find things to sell; he'll base it on the asset list you file with your paperwork. By the time he calculates the cost of an auction and subtracts his commission, the amount of time and expense it may take to hold that auction will likely not be worth it. In fact, in 96 percent of Chapter 7 cases, no assets are liquidated because they either are exempt or are not worth enough to bother selling.

If the bankruptcy trustee doesn't go after an asset, you get to keep it after the bankruptcy case is closed, as long as you accurately described it in your bankruptcy papers. If the U.S. Trustee audits your case and determines that you misrepresented the value of your assets, you could go to jail.

 Debt Dangers

The U.S. Trustee is a direct employee of the Department of Justice. Each of the 21 bankruptcy regional offices has a U.S. Trustee who oversees the work of the bankruptcy trustees. You likely won't ever meet the U.S. Trustee for your region unless the trustee questions your bankruptcy or does an audit and the U.S. Trustee follows up on the auditor's report.

Meeting Your Creditors

The first, and likely only, time you will meet your bankruptcy trustee face-to-face will be at the meeting of the creditors. You must attend this meeting if you don't want your case to be dismissed. The meeting is held at a hearing room of the federal building where the bankruptcy court is located, but you won't see a bankruptcy judge.

The only people who will attend this meeting likely will be you, your attorney, and the bankruptcy trustee, with any needed staff support. The trustee will ask you questions about your bankruptcy petition, your assets, and your tax returns. As long as all the paperwork is in order, this meeting will probably last less than an hour.

Some common questions include these:

- What do you make for a living?

- Where do you work?

- Are you living in your own house or apartment, or do you live with relatives?

- What are you doing to make ends meet?

- Have you made any recent large payments to other creditors, family members, or friends?

- Have you gotten any recent tax refunds?

- Did you give your attorney a list of all of your debts and all of your assets?

- Was that information true then? Is it true now?

- How did you arrive at the value of your home?

- Have you purchased a car within the past four months?

- Do you have the right to sue anyone for money?

The trustee will also ask questions related to the reason you state for filing bankruptcy. If your answers conflict with information in the bankruptcy petition, you will be asked about the conflicts. If you're represented by an attorney, the meeting will likely go faster than if you represent yourself. People who go before a trustee without an attorney face stiffer questioning about the information provided in the bankruptcy petition, as well as how they calculated their property exemptions.

Debt Dangers

If you choose to use a document preparer rather than an attorney, you will face the bankruptcy trustee alone. The document preparer will not be with you at the hearing.

Creditors rarely show up at these meetings. Most of the questions will come from the bankruptcy trustee. If the paperwork you submitted is complete and well prepared, the questions will be brief and the meeting quick and relatively painless.

Creditors show up at the meeting of the creditors primarily when they suspect that the debts you incurred were the result of a fraudulent act. For example, if you acquired a lot of debt just before filing for bankruptcy, that could be considered fraudulent behavior. Also, if the creditor believes you made false statements to get a loan, she could challenge the discharge of the debt.

If all your assets are exempt, you likely won't hear from the trustee again. But if there are nonexempt assets in your bankruptcy estate, the trustee may continue your case and set up another meeting. Between meetings, you could be asked to submit additional documentation about your assets. In a worst-case scenario, if the trustee thinks you may be hiding assets or income, he could refer your case to the U.S. Trustee.

If the trustee determines that he can seize and sell nonexempt assets, you will be expected to cooperate in getting them to the trustee. You also can negotiate to "buy back" the assets or substitute exempt assets for the nonexempt assets.

For example, suppose your state exempts up to $3,750 for household assets (as is true in the state of Alaska), but the exemption for jewelry is just $1,250. You decide you'd rather give up your household furnishings than a prized piece of jewelry. You may be able to negotiate a trade (although that's unlikely unless you have expensive household goods that could be sold to replace the money the trustee could get by selling the expensive piece of jewelry). The fact is, selling used furniture is expensive and rarely produces much profit.

The trustee usually won't ask to search your home to see if you are hiding any property, but if he does ask you to give him a guided tour of your home, you must cooperate. If you don't cooperate, the trustee can get a court order to force you to open your house to him.

If you owe back child support, the trustee is required to provide notice to whomever holds the child support claim, as well as the state child support agency. He also keeps them abreast of your case as it makes it through the bankruptcy courts. When the case is over, the child support agency and the person claiming child support will be given information about your last-known address, the last-known name and address of your employer, and the name of any creditor who holds a nondischargeable claim or claim that has been reaffirmed. Armed with this information, the state agency or people holding the support claim have the right to ask the creditors for your last-known address. Remember, back child support cannot be discharged as part of a bankruptcy filing.

When You Must See a Judge

In most Chapter 7 bankruptcy cases, filers never see a judge. You'll need to go before a judge only if a creditor or the trustee raises questions or you ask for an exception for special circumstances. Following are some common reasons you may end up before a judge:

- Your income level doesn't pass the means test for Chapter 7 and you want to ask for an exception for special circumstances.

- A creditor contests your right to discharge a particular debt.

- You want to ask the judge to discharge a debt that is not normally discharged in a Chapter 7 bankruptcy, such as a student loan or past-due taxes.

- You want to eliminate a lien on your property that would otherwise survive (remain against your property).

- You are handling your own bankruptcy and want to reaffirm a debt. For example, you want to keep your home and reaffirm the mortgage on that home. In this case, you keep paying the mortgage and keep the home as long as you meet the homestead exemption rules for your state.

Getting Rid of Your Debt

If you successfully complete the bankruptcy process and if there is no distribution to creditors, you will be able to discharge all otherwise dischargeable debts that existed on the day you filed bankruptcy, including:

- Bank credit cards

- Department and other retail store credit cards

- Doctor and hospital bills

- Loan balance due on loan deficiencies, such as money still due on a car that was repossessed or a home that was lost to foreclosure

- Mail-order and catalog purchases

- Most lawsuit judgments

- Personal loans

- Obligations under leases and contracts

- Utility bills

Debts that you cannot get discharged include these:

- Back child support and alimony

- Court-imposed fines and restitution

- Debts you owe because of a civil judgment from willful malicious acts or for personal injuries or death caused by your drunk driving

- Recent back taxes

- Student loans

- Unfiled taxes

I talk more about the process of clearing out debt and getting a fresh credit start in Chapter 9.

Attending the Required Budget-Counseling Sessions

Before getting the discharge, you will have to take a bankruptcy court–approved personal finance management course. Most likely, the agency that completed your required credit counseling will be able to provide this course. You will have to attend a budget-counseling course at an agency approved by the bankruptcy court.

Credit Cleaners

You can find an approved budget-counseling session by going to the U.S. Trustee website (www.usdoj. gov/ust/eo/bapcpa/ccde/ de_approved.htm).

The course must take at least two hours to meet the requirements of the bankruptcy court. Fees for the course are usually about $40. The agencies teaching the course do not have to be nonprofit, but they must offer you in-person services on a sliding fee scale.

When you complete the course, you will get a certificate showing you completed the course that you must file with the bankruptcy court before your case can be discharged. You must file this certificate no more than 45 days after your creditors meeting, so sign up to take the course as soon as you meet with the bankruptcy trustee.

Debt Dangers

If you don't complete the personal financial management course in time, the bankruptcy trustee can close your case without discharging your debts. You will then have to reopen your case, file the necessary forms, and request a discharge. So don't delay—take the course as soon as possible after your meeting with the creditors.

How Your Bankruptcy Case Ends

Your case will end with the discharge of all eligible debts. Your credit report should show that the debt has been discharged as part of a bankruptcy, but the creditor cannot indicate that you still owe money or are past due on payments. I talk more about how to repair your credit history in Chapter 13.

You can decide to change your mind in the middle of a bankruptcy filing and ask that the case be dismissed. In most cases, the court will do that without a problem, but if the trustee determines that withdrawal is not in the best interest of your creditors, he could oppose the withdrawal of your case. This could happen if you have significant nonexempt debts that could be seized and sold to satisfy your creditors. That's another reason to hire an attorney: if you have a lot of assets, you'll want to be sure you're filing in the appropriate way to keep those assets.

If you do decide to withdraw your case, you can file again, but you must wait at least 180 days to do so. You will have to pay a new filing fee and prepare new papers.

If the bankruptcy trustee determines that you must sell assets you want to keep, you may be able to convert your case to a Chapter 13 bankruptcy. You also can end up with a conversion to a Chapter 13 bankruptcy if the bankruptcy trustee determines that you don't pass the means test.

Now that we've taken a closer look at Chapter 7 bankruptcy, I focus on the details of filing under Chapter 13 bankruptcy laws in the next chapter.

The Least You Need to Know

- Your debts must be primarily personal debts to file for Chapter 7 bankruptcy, and you must pass the means test.

- You must get a certificate from a credit-counseling agency when you file for bankruptcy and get a certificate that you've taken a personal financial management course before your debts can be discharged.

- Your assets can be liquidated to pay off your creditors when filing a Chapter 7 bankruptcy unless they are protected by state homestead exemptions.

6

Chapter 13 Bankruptcy Process

In This Chapter

- ◆ Understanding eligibility requirements
- ◆ Developing a repayment plan
- ◆ Working with the trustee and creditors
- ◆ Seeing the judge
- ◆ Completing repayment and erasing debts

Chapter 13 enables you to reorganize your debts and keep your assets. While repaying your debts, you will be on a strict budget under the management of the bankruptcy trustee. In this chapter, we take a closer look at whether you're eligible and explore how to develop a repayment plan, the roles of the bankruptcy trustee and bankruptcy judge, and how a bankruptcy filing ends.

What Is Chapter 13?

A Chapter 13 bankruptcy plan is one in which you reorganize your debts, pay back part of them, and discharge the rest of them so you never have to pay them back. Shortly after or at the time of filing your Chapter 13 petition and schedule, you will develop a three- to five-year repayment plan, and as long as you can make the payments on your secured debt, you get to keep your most valuable property, especially your house and car.

A Chapter 13 bankruptcy can help you save valuable property that is not exempt, as long as you can afford to pay creditors based on a repayment plan that you work out with the bankruptcy trustee. You must have enough to pay for your necessities and keep up with the set Chapter 13 plan payments as well as payments specified by the plan to be paid directly. Throughout the term of your repayment plan, the bankruptcy court will control your financial life. You will not be able to buy and sell assets without the approval of the bankruptcy court.

Under the repayment plan, you will make payments to the bankruptcy trustee, who will decide how and when to pay your creditors.

Fulfilling the Counseling Requirement

As with Chapter 7 bankruptcy (see Chapter 5), before filing you must set up an appointment with a credit counselor (see Chapter 3) approved by the U.S. Trustee. After this appointment, you will get a certification to prove that you have attended the required credit-counseling session. In rare instances, the credit counselor will also develop a repayment plan, which you will have to file with your counseling certificate.

Meeting the Eligibility Requirements

Although passing the means test is the key eligibility requirement for Chapter 7 bankruptcy, you must consider some other eligibility requirements before filing for Chapter 13. These include prior bankruptcy discharges, types of debt, level of debt, and income tax filings.

Prior Bankruptcy Discharges

In the past, some people used bankruptcy discharges as a way to play cat-and-mouse with creditors who held a lien, such as a mortgage, against a secured piece of property, such as a house. They would periodically file bankruptcy to place a stay on the home to stop a fore-closure and then ask for the case to be dismissed once the foreclosure proceedings were stopped.

Today the bankruptcy law states that if you received a discharge in a previous Chapter 13 case in the last two years, or a discharge in a Chapter 7 case filed within the last four years, you can't get a Chapter 13 discharge.

You won't be barred from filing a Chapter 13 bankruptcy, but you can't get a debt discharge until the required time has passed. For example, suppose you were able to get most of your debt discharged under a Chapter 7 bankruptcy, but certain liens or debts could not be discharged by that case. You can then file a Chapter 13 bankruptcy to develop a repayment plan for any remaining debts. These remaining debts can't be discharged until you are at least four years away from the Chapter 7 discharge. This strategy of filing for Chapter 7 bank-ruptcy and then Chapter 13 bankruptcy is known as a Chapter 20 bankruptcy.

Businesses Aren't Eligible

If most of the debt you are trying to discharge is business debt, you can't use a Chapter 13 bankruptcy; you must file a Chapter 11 bank-ruptcy instead. Some people who are *sole proprietors* start a business by incurring debts for which they are primarily personally liable. If that is the case for you, you can use Chapter 13 bankruptcy to restructure debts.

def•i•ni•tion

> **Sole proprietors** are business-people who start a business by themselves, choosing to use neither the corporate nor the partnership form.

Debts Can't Be Too High

If your secured debts exceed $1,010,650 or your unsecured debts exceed $336,900, you must file a Chapter 11 bankruptcy. These debt levels are too high for a Chapter 13 bankruptcy.

Income Taxes Must Be Filed

When you file for a Chapter 13 bankruptcy, you must have completed all income tax filings that are due at both the federal and state level. You must provide evidence of these filings for the past four tax years when you file for bankruptcy. You can supply the bankruptcy trustee copies of the four years of tax filings or you can get copies of your returns from the IRS.

Your tax returns must be in the hands of the bankruptcy trustee before your first meeting with the creditors. That usually occurs about a month after you file, so if you're planning to file for bankruptcy and you don't have copies of your earlier tax returns, you should request them from the IRS as soon as possible after you decide to file.

If you haven't filed the returns, the trustee can keep the creditors meeting open for up to 120 days to give you time to file the returns. You can ask the bankruptcy court for an additional 120 days. But if you fail to submit these tax returns, your bankruptcy case will be dismissed.

Developing a Repayment Plan

As you pull together the required information, you can also start to develop a repayment plan. You will need to file this plan along with your bankruptcy petition. To be sure the bankruptcy judge will accept your plan, you need to follow these three steps:

◆ Step 1: Compute your disposable income.

◆ Step 2: Compare your disposable income to the debts you will have to pay in full in a Chapter 13 case. If you don't have enough disposable income to pay off these debts in full within five years, the judge will not confirm your plan.

◆ Step 3: If your plan pays all required debts, you must develop a plan that uses all additional disposable income to repay other debts within the appropriate time period. If not, the judge will not confirm your plan.

Let's go through the computations you must do to develop a plan that will be acceptable to a bankruptcy judge.

Compute Your Disposable Income

Before you can calculate your disposable income, you must determine whether your current monthly income figure is more or less than your state's median income. I show you how to do that in Chapter 4.

If your current monthly income is less than your state's family median income, you will be allowed to develop a three-year repayment plan. If your current monthly income is more than your state's median income, you must calculate your disposable income using IRS allowable expenses, which I discuss in Chapter 5. In that chapter, I take you through a four-step process to calculate disposable income.

 Credit Cleaners _____

Since the current monthly income figure is based on an average of the past six months, some bankruptcy courts base the income figure being used on actual rather than average income. The courts recognize that if someone has lost a job or is no longer able to work and has a much lower actual income, the debtor doesn't have a chance of completing a repayment plan. Check with your attorney to see if the local bankruptcy court is being more lenient on the income figures you must use.

Another big advantage for those whose current monthly income is below their state's median income is that you can use your actual expenses to calculate your disposable monthly income over a three-year period. Those with incomes above the state's median income must use the method shown in the means test, so you must use IRS-approved expenses. I show you those as part of the means test calculation in Chapter 5. I detail the allowable expenses in Step 2 of that test.

Although you can use a three-year repayment plan if your current monthly income is below your state's median income, you may not be able to make all your payments for secured debts, arrearages (past due date) and priority payments in that time. (I explain all these types of payments in Chapter 5.) If you can't pay all your secured debt payments plus all your arrearages and priority payments in a three-year period, you can ask the court to allow you to propose a longer five-year repayment plan.

If you earn more than your state's median monthly income, you must propose a five-year repayment plan. You cannot use the shorter three-year repayment window.

 Debt Dangers _____

> When developing your repayment plan and using actual expenses because your current monthly income is below the state's median income, don't make your expenses unreasonably low just to qualify for Chapter 13. Some people try to do this so they can keep property that might otherwise be lost in a Chapter 7 filing. If the court thinks your expenses are unreasonably low, your repayment plan can be rejected.

Whichever way you calculate your expenses (actual or IRS), you use that calculation of monthly expenses to determine your monthly disposable income. You subtract your expenses from your current monthly income to get your disposable income. Here's the calculation:

Current monthly income	$_____
Subtract actual or IRS expenses	($_____)
Monthly disposable income	$_____

Compare Your Disposable Income to Your Debts to Be Paid in Chapter 13

You must compute your monthly average secured debts, your monthly average arrearages, and your monthly average priority debts. I show you how to do this in Step 3 of the means test in Chapter 5. You must plan to repay all arrearages and all secured debts to hold on to property that you have used as collateral for a loan. Secured debt cannot be discharged unless you give up the property that is used as *collateral*.

def•i•ni•tion

Collateral is property that is pledged as security for a loan. For example, when you buy a house and agree to make monthly mortgage payments, you pledge that home as collateral. If you don't make the payments, the bank can foreclose on the home and take possession.

When you calculate these debts, you should calculate them on a 3-year (36-month) or a 5-year (60-month) basis. The steps in Chapter 5 are all based on a 60-month plan because, for Chapter 7 bankruptcy, you need to worry about disposable income only if your current monthly income is above your state's median income. With Chapter 13, you need to worry about disposable income whether or not your income exceeds the state's median income.

The key differences are that, for those whose income is less than the state's median income, actual expenses can be used when calculating disposable income and a repayment plan can be developed for just three years.

Those with current monthly income that is above the state's median income must use the stricter IRS expense guidelines and develop a repayment plan for five years.

However you calculated your expenses, you calculate your disposable income after debts that must be paid in this way:

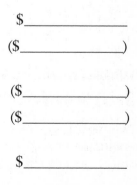

Monthly disposable income	$_____
Minus monthly average secured debts	($_____)
Minus average monthly payments on arrearages	($_____)
Minus monthly average priority debts	($_____)
Disposable income after secured debt, arrearages, and priority debt	$_____

Credit Cleaners _____

> Your repayment plan must cover any past-due child support or ali-
> mony, which are priority debts. But even if your support payments
> owed to a governmental unit cannot be paid in five years, the
> repayment plan can be approved. You will still owe the debt after
> bankruptcy. Back child support and alimony cannot be discharged with
> a bankruptcy.

If you still have enough income to pay your monthly average secured
debts, your monthly average priority debts, and your arrearages,
you've passed the first feasibility test for a Chapter 13 repayment plan.
If you don't have enough to cover these payments, you'll have to go
back to the drawing board. To file a repayment plan that a judge can
confirm, you must be able to pay these debts.

You can go back and rework your expenses, or you may need to decide
to give up some property that is secured by debt. An attorney can
help you sort through your income and expenses to develop a feasible
plan. If you don't have enough current income to support such a plan,
you may need to file for Chapter 7 bankruptcy.

Committing Disposable Income to Repayment of Other Debt

If after paying your mandatory debts (secured debts, arrearages, and
priority debts) you still have disposable income left, you will have to
commit all disposable income toward paying your other debts. If your
current monthly income is less than your state's median income, you
will have to commit all remaining disposable income to paying other
debts for three years. If your current monthly income is more than
your state's median income, you will have to commit all remaining
disposable income to paying other debts for five years.

Whichever category you fall into, you must develop your plan to show
how much of your other debt you can pay during your repayment
plan. Suppose you're eligible for a three-year plan but can't pay all
your mandatory debts in that time; you can ask for a five-year repayment plan instead.

If you have no disposable income after paying your mandatory debts, you can propose a repayment plan without paying any of your non-priority creditors, including credit card companies and hospital bills, as long as you have no nonexempt property. But the bankruptcy trustee could require you to sell some nonexempt assets to pay some of your debts. Your proposed repayment plan must provide for payments to creditors that would at least match what they would have gotten if you filed under Chapter 7.

 Debt Dangers

From the time you file for bankruptcy, your finances remain under the control of the bankruptcy trustee. You can't use funds or sell assets without the trustee's permission. You also must be ready to live under a strict budget for the duration of your repayment plan. If you can't do so, your bankruptcy case can be dismissed or be converted to a Chapter 7 bankruptcy.

Most bankruptcy filers don't have to worry about nonexempt property, but if you have a lot of equity in your home, this could become a major issue. For example, suppose you have $100,000 of nonexempt equity in your home. To save your home, your repayment plan would have to show you paying at least $100,000 to your unsecured creditors. Your plan must show that you are paying your unsecured creditors an amount at least equivalent to your nonexempt property. I talk more about exempt and nonexempt properties and saving your home in Chapter 8.

You may not be able to repay any of your unsecured creditors, but before your debts can be discharged, you must …

- ◆ Be current on all your federal and state income taxes.
- ◆ Be current on any child support or alimony.
- ◆ File your federal income tax annually with the court as you work through your repayment plan.
- ◆ File an annual income and expense statement with the court while you are still working your way through the repayment plan.

In addition to supplying the court with your income tax returns, you must give copies of those returns to creditors if they ask for them.

Filing Costs and Fees

Now that you have a plan in place, you're ready to file a bankruptcy petition. I highly recommend that you don't try this on your own, but if you plan to go solo without an attorney, you should at least pay a bankruptcy petition preparer to help you fill out the paperwork.

Credit Cleaners

You can take a look at the forms that you must file with the bankruptcy court by downloading them at the website of the U.S. Courts (www.uscourts.gov/bkforms/bankruptcy_forms.html).

You must pay a filing fee of $274 to file a bankruptcy petition. If you want an attorney to represent you, expect to spend between $2,400 and $4,000 in legal fees, which can be paid as part of your plan. If you just want help filling out the forms, that will cost you between $150 to $200 for a bankruptcy petition preparer.

What Property Is at Risk?

Unlike in a Chapter 7 bankruptcy filing, you won't be required to give up any property you own as long as you plan to repay debtors at least as much as they would have gotten under a Chapter 7 bankruptcy. For example, if all your property is exempt (see Appendix C) and you don't have enough disposable income to pay anything to unsecured creditors, you won't be forced to sell your property.

But if you have no disposable income to pay unsecured creditors and you have a lot of nonexempt property, you may be asked to sell property to pay at least some portion of the unsecured debt. The bankruptcy trustee and bankruptcy judge will make that decision. If you have a lot of nonexempt property, be sure to discuss this with your attorney before you file for bankruptcy.

Working with the Bankruptcy Trustee on Your Repayment Plan

The bankruptcy trustee for a Chapter 13 bankruptcy case has a different role than in a Chapter 7 bankruptcy case. You will get your first letter from the court about a week after you file. This letter will set the date for your 341 meeting, also known as the creditors meeting. Typically the Chapter 7 trustee is more concerned with assets, while the Chapter 13 trustee is more concerned with cash flow.

The trustee will make sure your repayment plan meets the technical requirements of the bankruptcy law and that it has a reasonable chance of succeeding. His pay is based on the fees charged each month to manage your repayment plan, so he has a vested interest in your being able to complete the plan. Most bankruptcy trustee fees are about 10 percent of the amount of your payment each month.

Bankruptcy trustees don't typically liquidate any property. They usually collect money from you each month you are in the repayment plan and dole out that money to creditors. Some trustees sponsor personal financial management courses, with the hope that you'll attend them and increase your chances of completing the repayment plan. If you're given the option, take the course. You've got nothing to lose.

Meeting Your Creditors

Your first meeting with the bankruptcy trustee will be about a month or two after you file your bankruptcy petition. This time period varies because some areas of the country are more backlogged than others. If you filed jointly with your spouse, both of you must attend the meeting. You will need to bring two forms of identification—a picture ID and government-issued proof of your Social Security number.

If all the paperwork is in order, the meeting will last less than 10 minutes. The trustee will briefly discuss your paperwork. No judge will be at the meeting, which will likely be held in a hearing room at the bankruptcy court.

Most of the discussion will center on the topic of your finances and whether you'll be able to successfully complete a repayment plan. The trustee will also check to be sure you filed tax returns for all taxable periods in the prior four years. If you haven't, the trustee will continue the creditors meeting until you file those returns. Your bankruptcy cannot move forward until the returns are filed.

When the bankruptcy trustee finishes asking questions, he will ask if any creditors want to question you. In most cases, unsecured creditors do not show up. But secured creditors could come if they object to how you've proposed to repay them as part of your repayment plan. If they do show up, they usually complain that you're proposing too long a time to pay them arrearages. Occasionally, unsecured creditors may show up and complain that your expenses are too high and you should cut expenses so you can pay more to unsecured creditors.

Expect that you may be required to negotiate with creditors. If you do make changes to the repayment plan after the meeting with the creditors, you will have to file a modified plan.

If you disagree with your creditors and don't negotiate, the trustee won't make a ruling on the issue. A bankruptcy judge must handle any objections made by creditors.

Seeing the Judge

You will be required to make at least one appearance before a bankruptcy judge before your repayment plan can be *confirmed* (approved). This is a called a confirmation hearing. At this hearing, the judge will either confirm your plan or send you back to the drawing board. You may or may not have to attend this hearing, depending on your attorney's instructions.

def•i•ni•tion

Confirmation is a ruling that the bankruptcy judge approves your Chapter 13 bankruptcy plan.

If the judge decides you don't have enough projected disposable income to at least pay your priority creditors in full and stay current on your secured debts, he can do one of two things:

- ◆ He can ask you to amend your proposed repayment plan and come back to court.

- ◆ He can decide that you don't have a chance of repaying the debt and dismiss the case.

Each time you make a change to your repayment plan, you must go before the bankruptcy judge for a confirmation. Since repayment plans take three to five years to complete and people's lives change a lot in that time period, you could be asking for modifications to the plan as your financial situation changes. But remember, to modify a plan, you must go back before the bankruptcy judge.

In addition to the confirmation hearing, you may need to see the bankruptcy judge if …

- ◆ You want to amend your plan for any reason.

- ◆ You want to pay less due on an asset than you owe. For example, the amount due on your car might be more than the car is worth. This may also be possible on your primary residence if Congress passes the "cramdown" law in 2009. More on that in Chapter 8.

- ◆ You need to respond to a trustee or creditor who asks that your case be dismissed.

- ◆ You need to respond to a creditor who protests the discharge of a particular debt.

- ◆ You want to ask the judge to discharge a debt that normally is not discharged because of special circumstances, such as discharging a student loan because of hardship.

- ◆ You want to ask the judge to eliminate a lien on your property that might otherwise survive bankruptcy.

- ◆ A mortgage company may file a Motion to Lift Stay, arguing that you have not maintained mortgage payments since you filed your case.

Possible Endings

Your Chapter 13 bankruptcy can end in one of four ways:

◆ You complete your repayment plan, and your remaining unsecured debt that qualifies is discharged. Some debts, such as student loans, can't be discharged unless you can prove hardship. Debts proved to be fraudulent also can't be discharged if the creditor convinces the court that you engaged in fraudulent activity, such as running up debts just before filing for bankruptcy. Debts that arise from criminal activity, drunk driving, and certain taxes can't be discharged, nor can debts arising from your willful or malicious acts.

◆ You are unable to complete your plan and you ask for a hardship discharge. Suppose that, as you're working through your repayment plan, you get sick, lose your job, or face some other hardship and can no longer make the payments. You may be able to seek a hardship discharge. If the court agrees with you about the reason for the hardship discharge, your unsecured debts will be discharged. But to keep your assets, you must be able to continue to pay what is due on the secured debts.

◆ You can ask to convert your Chapter 13 bankruptcy to a Chapter 7 bankruptcy because you realize that you can't complete your repayment plan. You may not be able to save all your assets if you go this route. That depends on whether your assets are exempt (see Appendix C). If you ask to convert your Chapter 13 case to a Chapter 7 bankruptcy, your secured debt treated under—and funded through—the plan will suddenly be subject to the original contract accounting. The car payment that was current in the context of your Chapter 13 plan may be one and a half years past due under the context of your original installment contract. The original contract will come back into play under Chapter 7.

♦ You ask for your bankruptcy case to be dismissed, or the trustee or creditor successfully moves that your case be dismissed. You will still owe your creditors the balances on your debts before you filed for bankruptcy, minus any payments you made as part of your repayment plus any accrued interest. If your case is dismissed, the credit bureaus will note the case filing for 10 years from the date of filing. A discharged filing will be noted for only seven years from the date of filing.

Making it through a Chapter 13 bankruptcy requires a lot of discipline. You must live on a strict budget for the entire three- to five-year period. About 65 percent of the people who file for Chapter 13 do not successfully complete their repayment plan. So be ready for a lot of hard work and sacrifices to get through it. But if you've chosen this route over a Chapter 7 filing to save assets, you'll be glad you pushed your way through what will be one of the most difficult periods of your life. You truly will get a fresh financial start and still keep what you had before starting the bankruptcy.

Now let's look at which bankruptcy may be best for you based on your financial circumstances.

The Least You Need to Know

♦ Chapter 13 bankruptcy allows you to reorganize your debts and keep your assets.

♦ You must develop a three- or five-year repayment plan that a bankruptcy judge must approve.

♦ Your financial life will be under the control of the bankruptcy trustee throughout the life of a Chapter 13 bankruptcy.

Chapter 7

Choosing the Right Type of Bankruptcy

In This Chapter

- ◆ Pros and cons of Chapter 7
- ◆ Pros and cons of Chapter 13
- ◆ When to use other bankruptcy types
- ◆ Rules for upper-income filers

I give you the pros and cons of each type of bankruptcy filing, but everyone's financial situation is different. Before you decide which type to file, sit down with a bankruptcy attorney and discuss your options. In some cases, it will be an easy decision, but most people weigh both emotional and financial issues as they choose the right type of bankruptcy for them. In this chapter, I talk about the pros and cons of filing each type of personal bankruptcy and discuss the special rules for upper-income filers.

Why Choose Chapter 7?

Chapter 7 bankruptcy likely will be your best choice if you meet the eligibility requirements and don't have nonexempt assets for the trustee to seize (see Appendix C). Most people don't lose their homes as long as they make their mortgage payment, because of homestead exemption rules. These exemption rules are based on state laws. (I talk more about saving your home in Chapter 8.) But you can't choose Chapter 7 bankruptcy if you received a bankruptcy discharge in the past eight years.

Your mortgage and house payments must be current when you file for Chapter 7 bankruptcy, and you must reaffirm those debts to keep them. If you don't, you will have to give them up. You'll lose secured debts (such as a home that is used as collateral for a mortgage, or a car that serves as collateral for a car loan) if you can't make the payments.

Pros of Filing for Chapter 7 Bankruptcy

The primary benefits of filing Chapter 7 include these:

- All your unsecured debt can be erased, and there's no limit to how much debt can be discharged.

- Neither your creditors nor the bankruptcy court can touch any wages or property that you acquire after the date you file for bankruptcy. You'll learn more about what is in your bankruptcy estate in Chapter 4.

- Your case is usually over in three to six months and your unsecured debts are gone.

- As long as you are up-to-date on your mortgage and car payments, you can usually keep both.

- State and federal exemption rules allow you to keep most necessities, such as household furniture and clothing (see Appendix C).

- You won't be under the control of the bankruptcy court for three to five years, working through a repayment plan.

When you emerge from Chapter 7, you are debt free except for the loans you reaffirm, such as your mortgage. Certain types of debts do survive Chapter 7, including student loans, recent taxes, and back child support. Also, you must repay loans owed to a pension plan, or they will be considered withdrawals from that plan and you could owe taxes and penalties.

Debt Dangers

You can't ask the judge to erase debts for personal injuries or death from your drunk driving. A creditor can also file a court order asking the judge not to discharge debts incurred by your fraudulent actions, such as running up debt on credit cards just before filing.

Cons of Filing for Chapter 7 Bankruptcy

The biggest disadvantage of filing Chapter 7 bankruptcy is that you can lose any nonexempt property if the trustee believes he can sell it and get money to pay your creditors. Other disadvantages include the following:

♦ If you're facing foreclosure and can't bring your payments up-to-date, a Chapter 7 bankruptcy can only stall your foreclosure, not stop it.

♦ If you are a cosigner on a loan, the other person or people on that loan will be stuck with the debt. You could lose friends or family if they must repay your debt.

♦ You can file for Chapter 7 bankruptcy only once over eight years.

♦ A Chapter 7 bankruptcy stays on your credit report for 10 years. Although you won't be denied credit for that long, it will take at least three to four years to rebuild your credit score. I talk more about recovery from bankruptcy in Part 4.

♦ Once you file, you may find it difficult to withdraw your case. The bankruptcy trustee could determine that it's in the best interest of your creditors to continue the case, especially if he has found assets that could be sold to satisfy creditors.

Credit Cleaners

Always be certain to carefully list all the assets that you own and check with family members to be sure you're not listed on a family asset. You may be a co-owner of a family asset with your siblings and not even know your parents set that up.

If you have any doubts about whether you can repay your debts, you should choose to file under Chapter 7. If you start your case as a Chapter 13 bankruptcy and then find out that you are unable to complete the repayment plan, all the money you paid toward your debts will be lost. So it's best to just start with a Chapter 7 bankruptcy if you have doubts about your ability to make payments.

Why Choose Chapter 13?

The biggest advantage of filing under Chapter 13 of the bankruptcy code is that you get to keep all your exempt and nonexempt assets. If you're behind in your mortgage and car payments but you want to keep the assets, a Chapter 13 bankruptcy can buy you the time to catch up on those payments and keep the assets. Since you'll have to pay less, or possibly nothing, on your unsecured debts, you can use that extra cash to catch up on your past-due payments. You generally cannot do that with a Chapter 7 bankruptcy filing.

Another big advantage of a Chapter 13 filing is that if an asset, such as your car, is worth much less than you owe, the bankruptcy judge can lower your car loan principal to the current value of the car. You must have purchased the car at least $2\frac{1}{2}$ years ago to take advantage of this part of the bankruptcy law.

Some other good reasons to choose a Chapter 13 bankruptcy over a Chapter 7 bankruptcy include these:

♦ You owe money in back taxes, are in arrears on a student loan, or must pay other debt (such as debt arising from a drunk driving claim) that you want to pay off over time.

- You want to repay your debts that cannot be erased, but you need more time to do so.

- You have debts that can be discharged only under Chapter 13. These include marital debts from a divorce settlement arrangement; debts incurred to pay a nondischargeable tax debt; court fees; condominium, cooperative, or homeowner's association fees; debts for loans from a retirement plan; and debts that couldn't be discharged in a previous bankruptcy.

Pros of Filing for Chapter 13 Bankruptcy

The pros of filing for a Chapter 13 bankruptcy include these:

- You get to keep all your property, provided that you can successfully complete the repayment plan.

- You can get a longer time to pay the debt.

- You can pay back taxes over a three- to five-year period, and you may even be able to pay them without interest or penalties (see Chapter 9 for more information about paying off taxes).

- Debts that you could not get discharged in a Chapter 7 bankruptcy can be paid off over time with a Chapter 13 bankruptcy. For example, suppose you must pay a claim for personal injury caused when drunk driving: Chapter 13 can buy you time to repay that debt over three or five years.

- You are protected from creditors' collection efforts, such as wage garnishment, foreclosure, or repossession of property, as long as you continue to make payments to your confirmed Chapter 13 repayment plan.

- Your creditors can't go after cosigners on a loan, as long as your repayment plan provides for full repayment of that loan.

- You can stretch out payments on your overdue alimony and child support.

◆ You can buy time to get caught up on your mortgage and car payments so you can keep the assets.

◆ You can get some relief from creditors even if you got debt relief under a Chapter 7 bankruptcy fewer than eight years ago.

◆ If you can't make the repayments, you can back out of the filing. Under Chapter 7, you need the permission of the court to have your case dismissed. If you do back out, you can't file again for 180 days.

Cons of Filing for Chapter 13 Bankruptcy

The biggest disadvantage of filing for Chapter 13 bankruptcy is that your financial life is totally under the control of the bankruptcy trustee throughout the time of your repayment plan. You can't buy or sell assets without his permission. Since one's life situation can change a lot over a three- or five-year period, such as a job change or health problem, you can't make any moves without first talking with your trustee.

Most people find that giving up their financial freedom for three to five years is difficult. You will have to live on a very strict budget during the time of your repayment plan.

The other cons of filing a Chapter 13 bankruptcy include these:

◆ You must use your disposable debt to pay all unsecured debt, so you have to live on a strict budget meager enough to avoid objections to confirmation by creditors or by the bankruptcy trustee.

◆ Legal fees are high for a Chapter 13 bankruptcy because it's more complex to develop a repayment plan acceptable to the bankruptcy court—plus, the case goes on for the entire length of your repayment plan (three or five years). During that time, there could be numerous court hearings.

◆ You may not be able to successfully complete a Chapter 13 repayment plan, and all money paid toward debts is lost. Had you filed for Chapter 7, those debts that were unsecured would have been discharged without you having to make any payments.

Using a Chapter 20 Bankruptcy

Although there's no official Chapter 20 bankruptcy in the bankruptcy code, you can legitimately start your process of getting a fresh financial start by filing a Chapter 7 bankruptcy, having all your unsecured debt discharged, and then filing a Chapter 13 to get additional time to pay off the debts that cannot be discharged.

Some debts can't be discharged with a Chapter 7 bankruptcy, such as these:

♦ Debts incurred to pay nondischargeable taxes

♦ Court-imposed fines

♦ Back child support and alimony

♦ Debts owed under marital settlement agreements

♦ Loans owed to a pension plan

♦ Student loans

♦ Debts for personal injury or death resulting from drunk driving

You can then file a Chapter 13 bankruptcy to get the debts discharged or buy time to repay them. These debts cannot be discharged under Chapter 7 but can be discharged under Chapter 13:

♦ Debts incurred to pay nondischargeable taxes

♦ Court-imposed fines

♦ Debts owed under marital settlement agreements

♦ Loans owed to a pension plan

Your other debts were discharged under Chapter 7; you can repay the remaining debt that can't be discharged under Chapter 13 with a three- to five-year repayment plan. This way, by using Chapter 20, you can stop any attempt by the remaining creditors to seek a judgment in court, garnish your wages, or undertake other collection activities. This buys you more time to pay down the debt.

Why Consider Alternatives?—Chapters 11 and 12

If most of your debt is business debt or you run a family farm or fishing business, you don't qualify for Chapter 13 bankruptcy. You can use the business type of Chapter 7 bankruptcy if you want to liquidate the business, but if you plan to keep the business after reorganizing your debt, you then must file under Chapter 11 or 12. Chapter 11 is for reorganizing the debt of business organizations. Chapter 12 is for reorganizing the debt of family farmers and fishermen.

Chapter 11

If your debts primarily come from operating a business, your secured debts exceed $1,010,650, or your unsecured debts total more than $336,900 in a case commenced before April 1, 2010 (after that time, the dollar amount could be adjusted for inflation), you must file under Chapter 11 of the bankruptcy code.

Chapter 11 bankruptcy is much more complex and costly to file. The initial filing fee is $839, plus you must pay a quarterly fee based on a percentage of the disbursements made to pay your debts. The fee runs from $250 a quarter (when disbursements total less than $15,000) to $10,000 per quarter (for disbursements over $5 million). The fee must be paid until the bankruptcy court either approves your reorganization plan or dismisses your case.

Attorney fees are much higher, too. Most attorneys require a retainer fee of $7,500 or more just to handle a Chapter 11 bankruptcy. Court fees on top of that retainer can range from $1,000 to $10,000.

> **Credit Cleaners**
>
> If you think Chapter 11 is the best choice, given your special circumstances, be sure to pick an attorney who has a lot of experience filing Chapter 11 bankruptcies. Don't try to save money by using an attorney whose practice primarily helps consumers file bankruptcy.

If you own a small business
and do need to file bankruptcy,
Chapter 11 gives you the mecha-
nism to restructure the debt load
of that business. For example,
you can restructure your debt
and give lenders priority on your
business's earnings to erase some
of the debt or get more favorable
repayment terms.

Credit Cleaners

If your business is in
financial trouble, filing
Chapter 11 can stop all
credit collections using an
automatic stay. The automatic
stay requires all creditors to
cease collection attempts.

The bankruptcy court may also permit you to reject or cancel contracts to erase debt burden, such as a lease for equipment. You'll also
be protected from other litigation against the business through the
imposition of an automatic stay. While an automatic stay is in place,
most litigation against you is put on hold until it can be resolved in
bankruptcy court or resumed after your business emerges from bankruptcy in its original venue.

If your business debts exceed your business's assets, the bankruptcy
restructuring can result in your business being left with nothing and
your company owned by your creditors. So if you do file for Chapter
11 bankruptcy, be sure you understand the risks that you're taking.

Any plan you devise to reorganize your company's debt must be heard
before a bankruptcy judge. The court is the ultimate party responsible
for determining whether or not your proposed plan of reorganization
complies with bankruptcy law.

What a Chapter 11 bankruptcy may allow you to do after reorganization is keep your business, rather than liquidating it as part of a
business Chapter 7. Some debtors can emerge from Chapter 11 bankruptcy in a matter of months, and some may be under bankruptcy
court supervision for years. It all depends on the size and complexity
of the bankruptcy.

A plan for reorganization can be proposed by any party with an interest in the business. Debtors are usually given about 120 days to come
up with a satisfactory plan for reorganizing the debt. After that time

elapses, creditors can propose their own reorganization plan. A plan must be voted on and approved by the creditors.

If a plan cannot be developed that is approved by the creditors, the bankruptcy court can either convert the case to a liquidation under Chapter 7, or if it's in the best interests of the creditors and the bankruptcy estate, the case can be dismissed. If the case is dismissed, everything goes back to the way it was prior to the bankruptcy filing. Creditors will then need to satisfy their claims using nonbankruptcy laws.

Chapter 12 Bankruptcy

Chapter 12 is a special type of bankruptcy for family farmers and fishermen. Congress developed special rules for these types of businesses because they play a unique role in our society and economy.

If you qualify for Chapter 12 bankruptcy, you'll get most of the benefits of Chapter 13, plus a few more. Your repayment plan is not restricted to five years and you have more leeway in how you can restructure your mortgage—this is because, in most cases, your mortgage is not only on your home, but also on the land for your farm. The debts that can be discharged are based on the debt-discharge rules for Chapter 7 bankruptcy.

To qualify for this special type of bankruptcy, as a family farmer, your debts cannot exceed $3.2 million. At least 50 percent of your debts (excluding your home mortgage) must come from farming operations. Also, at least 50 percent of your income must come from farming operations.

To qualify as a family fisherman, your debts cannot exceed $1.5 million. At least 80 percent of those debts (not including your home mortgage) must come from commercial fishing operations. Also, at least 50 percent of your income must come from commercial fishing operations.

The fee for filing a Chapter 12 case is $230. If you do qualify for Chapter 12 bankruptcy, work with an attorney who specializes in Chapter 12 cases to get all the protections the law allows.

Special Rules for Upper-Income Filers

If you make considerably more than the median income for your state, you most likely will not qualify for consumer Chapter 7 bankruptcy. Read Chapters 4 and 5 to find out the eligibility requirements for Chapter 7 bankruptcy.

You can owe too much to file for Chapter 13. If you owe more than $1,010,650 in unsecured debts or more than $336,900 in secured debts in a case commenced before April 1, 2010 (the upper limits could be adjusted for inflation), you cannot use Chapter 13; you must use Chapter 11.

When the new bankruptcy law was passed, Congress believed that there were a lot of "can pay" debtors who would be forced into the more expensive Chapter 11. They wanted to deny these "can pay" debtors access to Chapter 7 and Chapter 13 bankruptcies by instituting the new income-based eligibility requirements under the means test.

Immediately after the bill was first passed, the number of people filing for bankruptcy plunged because they thought they could not qualify for bankruptcy. But a sampling of bankruptcy filers after the passage of the 2005 law proved that those advocates who claimed that high-income filers would be driven from the system were wrong. Advocates expected there would be fewer people of modest means filing for bankruptcy.

In promoting the law, for example, advocates said that 800,000 filers in 2007 alone would be driven from the bankruptcy courts because they were high-income deadbeats.

Credit Cleaners _____

You may hear the term high-income deadbeat and think you make too much money to file for bankruptcy, but don't believe it unless you've talked with a bankruptcy attorney who has told you that you don't qualify. Means testing is a complicated process, and attorneys have software to help sort out whether or not you are eligible.

That's not what happened. In reality, few people were driven away from being eligible for bankruptcy. Those filing bankruptcy were found to be everyday Americans in serious financial distress, not deadbeat high-income filers.

Debtors filing for bankruptcy in 2007 had even greater debt loads than their counterparts from 2001. This should be no surprise to anyone, because we know there was a national trend of increasing consumer debt until everything imploded in 2008 and 2009.

So the tale that was told by advocates for the 2005 bankruptcy reform bill did not eliminate high-income deadbeats. That was a fantasy they developed to get the bill passed. Instead, the new bill was a general assault on all debtors, regardless of their financial circumstances.

Now because of the fears regarding the eligibility requirements of the new bill, debtors are waiting longer—and incurring more debt—before ultimately seeking bankruptcy relief. Don't buy into those fears.

If you are drowning in debt, consult with a bankruptcy attorney to assess your eligibility, as well as your risk of losing assets. You may find bankruptcy is the right prescription to repair your financial mess.

Now that you know the pros and cons of filing for the various types of personal bankruptcies, let's take a closer look at how you can use bankruptcy to save your home.

The Least You Need to Know

◆ A Chapter 7 bankruptcy ends the fastest, but you risk losing nonexempt property. If you're not current on your mortgage and you want to affirm your debt, you can lose your home.

◆ Chapter 13 helps you buy time to get caught up on your mortgage and car payments so you can keep both your exempt and nonexempt property.

◆ If your debts are primarily business debts and you want to reorganize those debts, you need to file Chapter 11.

◆ If your debts primarily come from farming or fishing, you may choose to file under Chapter 12.

Part 3

Using Bankruptcy for Specific Goals

In this part, I explore how you can use bankruptcy to save your home, get a fresh financial start, clear out medical debt, and clean up a financial mess after a divorce.

Chapter 8

Saving Your Home

In This Chapter

- ◆ Halting foreclosure
- ◆ Using the homestead exemption
- ◆ Applying equity reduction
- ◆ Making use of law changes to more easily keep your home

Your home may be the most crucial asset you can save when filing for bankruptcy. Hopefully you won't wait until you get that final foreclosure notice taped to your door to take action to save your home, but even if you do, bankruptcy can stall foreclosure proceedings and, depending on your finances, possibly save your home.

In this chapter, I focus on how foreclosure works and how you can use bankruptcy to stall that foreclosure. Then once you've stalled the foreclosure, you might be able to use bankruptcy to save your home.

Bankruptcy Filing to Stop Foreclosure

When you see a warning taped to your door or form letters from investors or bankruptcy attorneys indicating an auction and upcoming sale of your home, you no longer have time to wait. Get thee to an attorney and file for bankruptcy if you want to save your home.

def•i•ni•tion

A **dispossessory action** is a demand that you leave your property after a lender has foreclosed on the property, which you no longer own. A lender will file this action as part of the eviction process.

Foreclosure is the means by which your lender can legally repossess (take ownership of) your home if you aren't making payments on your mortgage. Once the lender forecloses on your home, you must move out of the home or you will be evicted, usually after a so-called *dispossessory action* is filed in the state court.

In addition to losing your home, you could owe the lender more money. This happens if the value of your home is less than the amount you owe on your mortgage loan. In such a case, your property would likely be auctioned to the highest bidder by the county sheriff or some other officer of the court. Often the lender bids on the house at the auction, at the price of the debt owed. If no other buyer bids higher, the bank wins the property.

But realistically, you shouldn't wait for that moment to get your financial life together. As soon as you miss your first payment on your home, talk with a housing counselor to see if you can modify the terms of your loan so that you can afford to pay the mortgage.

Credit Cleaners

You can find a housing counselor by going to the website of the U.S. Department of Housing and Urban Development (HUD), at www.hud.gov/foreclosure. There you will find information about seeking help to avoid foreclosure, as well as information about local counselors who can help you.

The first step in the process of loan foreclosure is to send a Notice of Default (for a nonjudicial foreclosure) or file a lawsuit (for a judicial foreclosure) in the county where the property is located. If you live in a state that allows nonjudicial foreclosure, you then enter into a re-instatement period, which is a period of about three months before your home is sold by the trustee or lender at auction. Each state sets its own rules on how long the process of foreclosure can take.

If you don't pay the amount due in full on the mortgage payments you missed during the reinstatement period or work out some other payment arrangement with your trustee or lender, a Notice of Trustee Sale is recorded and sent to you. This notice gives the date, time, and location of the sale of your property.

If your state requires a judicial foreclosure process, your lender will need to start a court action to repossess your property. This type of foreclosure is required when a trust deed or mortgage does not have a "power of sale" clause, which means the lender must take the borrower to court. This can be a much more lengthy and costly process than a nonjudicial foreclosure.

The judicial foreclosure process starts when a lender files a lawsuit to foreclose and names the borrower in default as the defendant. Once the lender has filed a lawsuit, the borrower and any other defendants usually have 20 days to reply formally to the lawsuit and present their case.

If there is no reply to the suit, the judge rules against the defendant and orders that the mortgage or deed of trust be foreclosed on and the property be sold at auction. So if you get a notice that a lawsuit or *lis pendens* has been filed with the county, get thee to an attorney quickly.

def•i•ni•tion

Lis pendens, which in Latin means "suit pending," is a written notice that a lawsuit has been filed concerning real estate. The lawsuit can involve either the title to the property or a claimed ownership interest in that property. The notice is commonly filed in the county land records office during a foreclosure process.

Your attorney will reply to the lawsuit on your behalf, and a court hearing date will be set. The timing of this hearing varies by state and depends on the backlog of cases. When the case is heard in court, the judge either will order that the loan be foreclosed on or will dismiss the case.

If the judge rules against you and orders the loan to be foreclosed on, the public foreclosure auction sale will be scheduled by the county sheriff or by some other party designated for that purpose by the county where the property is located.

Public foreclosure auction sales are advertised in the local paper. The property will be sold to the highest bidder at the auction; if there are no acceptable bids from the auction participants, the lender will take back the property. The judge may also award the lender a deficiency judgment against the borrower if the bid that is accepted is less than the amount owed.

Saving Your Home from Foreclosure

Now that you know how you can lose your home to foreclosure, let's focus on how to *save* that home. When you file for bankruptcy, the foreclosure process stops with an automatic stay.

If you file for Chapter 7 bankruptcy, your mortgage payments must be up-to-date to save the home. But if you file for Chapter 13 bankruptcy, you can buy extra time to bring your payments up-to-date using a repayment plan. So if you're trying to save your home and you're late on your payments, you probably want to use Chapter 13.

You cannot discharge (erase) the amount you owe on your home if you want to keep your home. Home mortgages are secured loans, which means you put up your home as collateral to borrow money from the bank. The bank gets to take possession of that collateral if you don't make the payments. The best you can do when filing Chapter 7 bankruptcy is to stop foreclosure proceedings and use the time to catch up your payments. A common technique is to use a bankruptcy to stop the foreclosure process. You then buy time to work out your mortgage payments in arrears outside the Chapter 7 process before the bank can lift the stay and foreclose on the home.

Whether or not you get to keep your home depends on the type of bankruptcy you file and the homestead exemption rules in your state. *Homestead exemptions*, depending on your state, allow you to keep your home even if you have equity built up in that home.

How do you figure out how much equity you have in your home? You need two key numbers:

def•i•ni•tion

A **homestead exemption** is the amount of equity you have in your primary residence that is protected from bankruptcy. Each state sets its own rules on how much you can claim as a homestead exemption.

- The price at which your home could sell today, which is known as the market value. If you're not sure what homes are selling for in your area, you can talk to a Realtor or find estimated prices on Zillow (www.zillow.com).

- The amount you still owe to the bank on your mortgage. If you have more than one mortgage or an equity line, you should include the balances from every loan for which you used your home as collateral.

When you have these numbers, you can calculate your home's equity:

Market value of your home	$_____
Subtract your mortgage total	($_____)
Equity in your home	$_____

If you owe more than your home is worth, you have a loan that is underwater.

Understanding Homestead Exemptions

Now that you know the amount of equity in your home, you can determine whether a Chapter 7 bankruptcy can save your home. If the homestead exemption in your state (see Appendix C) is less than the amount of equity in your home, a bankruptcy trustee can sell your home and use the equity to pay off other debts.

For example, the homestead exemption in the state of Alabama is $5,000. Suppose your home is worth $150,000 and you owe just $100,000 on your mortgage. That means you have $45,000 that can be used to pay down debt and $5,000 that you would get to keep if your house were sold. (This example simplifies the calculation, because some money would be paid out in selling costs of the home.)

If you have more equity in your home than the homestead exemptions allow, you probably should consider filing for Chapter 13 bankruptcy. I also talk shortly about other strategies you can use to save your home even if you don't have a large enough homestead exemption. The reason Chapter 13 may work better for you is that no matter how much equity you have in your home, if you can maintain both your Chapter 13 plan payments and due mortgage installments paid directly to the bank after the case filing, you can save your home.

Each state sets its own rules on homestead exemptions. Seven states protect an unlimited dollar amount of your primary residence with their homestead exemptions, as long as your lot size meets the state requirements. These include Arkansas, Florida, Iowa, Kansas, Oklahoma, South Dakota, and Texas. The District of Columbia doesn't officially have a homestead exemption, but it also protects an unlimited value of your primary residence.

Eight states set their homestead rules based on both a dollar limit and lot size. These states include Alabama, Hawaii, Louisiana, Michigan, Minnesota, Mississippi, Nebraska, and Oregon.

Three states offer no homestead exemption: Maryland, New Jersey, and Pennsylvania. New Jersey and Pennsylvania do allow you to use the federal homestead exemption rules, which allows up to $20,200 to be exempted in equity.

All other states use a homestead exemption rule based on equity only. Most states do require that you reside in the home as your primary residence before you can take advantage of the homestead exemption rules. Homestead exemption laws do not protect second homes, vacation homes, or other real estate in which you aren't living when you file.

Declaration of Homestead

In most states, the homestead exemption rule kicks in automatically when you file for bankruptcy, but nine states require you to declare your homestead exemption before filing. States in which you must declare your homestead exemption include Alabama, Idaho, Massachusetts, Montana, Nevada, Texas, Utah, Virginia, and Washington.

Wildcard Exemptions

Some states offer wildcard exemptions that let you increase the amount of your homestead exemption, if that's the way you decide to use the wildcard. Wildcard exemptions allow you to keep a certain dollar amount of assets. You decide which assets you want to use it to save.

Fourteen states have wildcard rules that can increase your homestead exemption. These include California, Connecticut, Georgia, Indiana, Kentucky, Maine, Maryland, Missouri, New Hampshire, Ohio, Pennsylvania, Vermont, Virginia, and West Virginia. If your state allows you to use the federal exemption rules, you may have a wildcard available as well.

Tenancy by the Entirety

Married couples have an advantage over unmarried couples in states that allow tenancy by the entirety. If you live in one of these states and hold your title by *tenancy by the entirety*, your home's value can be protected 100 percent if only one spouse owes the debt.

Seventeen states (and the District of Columbia) allow spouses to own property by tenancy by the entirety. These include Delaware, Florida, Hawaii, Illinois, Indiana, Maryland, Massachusetts, Michigan, Missouri, North Carolina, Ohio, Pennsylvania, Rhode Island, Tennessee, Vermont, Virginia, and Wyoming.

Relocation, New Home Purchase, and Bankruptcy Filing

If you bought your current home at least 40 months before you file for bankruptcy, you can take full advantage of your state's homestead exemption. If you moved within the same state, even if you own your current home for less than 40 months, you can still use your state's homestead exemption without restrictions.

Debt Dangers

If you have moved recently or plan to move soon, time your bankruptcy filing very carefully. Your homestead exemptions may be at risk if you move within two years of a bankruptcy filing.

But if you bought your home within 40 months of filing with proceeds from the sale of another home in another state, your homestead exemption may be restricted. As long as you lived in the new state for at least two years, you can use the state's homestead exemption, subject to a cap of $136,875.

If you moved to your current state less than two years ago, you must use the homestead exemption available in the state where you made your home for the 180 days prior to the two-year period before filing for bankruptcy, and it will be subject to a $136,875 cap. In other words, the government doesn't want you to move to a state with a higher homestead exemption just before filing for bankruptcy. People were doing this to protect assets by buying homes in states with an unlimited dollar amount in homestead exemptions.

This punishment for moving hits people particularly hard if they live in one state with a high-dollar homestead exemption and move to another state with a high-dollar homestead exemption. Even with this scenario, their homestead exemption will be capped at $136,875. For example, both Texas and Florida have unlimited-value homestead exemptions. But if you move between these two states within 40 months of filing, your homestead exemption will be capped by $136,875 even if it would have been unlimited if you hadn't moved.

So if you're in trouble financially and are thinking of moving, talk with an attorney about your homestead exemption rules. You may want to delay the move and file for bankruptcy to clear out debts before the move. But you may have trouble getting a mortgage in your new location after filing for bankruptcy. As long as you have enough cash to put down, you'll probably be able to get a mortgage within two to three years of filing bankruptcy. I talk more about buying a house after bankruptcy in Chapter 15.

Illegal Act and Homestead Exemptions

Sometimes you can lose your rights to use a homestead exemption if you commit certain crimes or deceive creditors. Even if your state allows an unlimited dollar homestead exemption, your rights to use that exemption could be limited if you engage in certain types of misconduct.

If you committed a felony, a securities violation, or certain crimes that led to death or serious bodily injury, your homestead exemption could be limited to $136,875. This depends on how the court interprets your circumstances.

The bankruptcy court can lift your cap if it determines that the homestead in question is reasonably necessary for you to support yourself and your family. You will need an attorney to represent you before the judge and help you make the case to save your homestead exemption.

> **Debt Dangers**
>
> If you were involved in an illegal act, your homestead exemption could be limited when you file for bankruptcy. Be sure to discuss any legal problems you may have in your past with your bankruptcy attorney before filing your case.

Even if you didn't commit a crime, a bankruptcy court can limit your homestead exemption if it determines that you cheated your creditors. For example, if you disposed of nonexempt property with the intent to hinder, delay, or defraud your creditors, the bankruptcy court could cap your homestead exemption. If you are planning to file for bankruptcy, consult an attorney before disposing of any assets, to preserve your homestead exemption rights and protect your home.

Options If You Have Too Much Equity in Your Home

You may still want to file for Chapter 7 bankruptcy if you have too much equity in your home. You can consider a number of strategies:

- ◆ Refinance your home so you owe more than you currently do. This strategy may be very difficult if you already have a low credit score. Also, I don't recommend this strategy unless it results in a lower mortgage payment. You may be able to lower your mortgage payment if you can lower your interest rate and reduce the amount you must pay each month. Remember, bankruptcy can't save your home if you can't make the mortgage payments.

- ◆ Sell some nonexempt assets to pay the trustee the same amount he's hoping to get out of the sale of your house. You will need to sell assets or use income you earned after filing for bankruptcy. You cannot use anything in your bankruptcy estate at the time of filing. (I talk about the bankruptcy estate in Chapter 4.)

- ◆ Take out a home equity line to pay off the debts you won't be able to discharge with a Chapter 7 bankruptcy, such as back child support or alimony, back taxes, or a student loan.

 Credit Cleaners

Senior citizens can be hit hard by the homestead exemption rules because they can have a lot of equity in a home they bought 25 or 30 years ago. One option for seniors who are over the age of 62 is a reverse mortgage. You can find out more about the pros and cons of reverse mortgages at AARP's website (www.aarp.org/money/personal/reverse_mortgages/). With a reverse mortgage, you get a monthly payment to help you afford to live and pay off debts; you don't have to pay off the mortgage.

If none of these strategies work for you, your best bet is to file Chapter 13 bankruptcy, to save your home if you have a lot of equity in your home.

If you're planning to use any money you get from a refinance to pay off debt, you must do so 90 days before filing for bankruptcy. If you pay $600 or more to a regular creditor 90 days before filing, you could be giving preferential treatment to a creditor, which is a big no-no in the eyes of the bankruptcy court. If you're thinking of paying a relative or close friend before filing for bankruptcy, you must do that a year before filing; otherwise, you'll get in trouble with the court. A bankruptcy judge can ask your family member or friend to repay the money if you paid off the loan less than 12 months ago.

New Bankruptcy Laws and Saving Your Home

If you owe more on your home than it is worth, sometime in the future you may be able to count on a law that has passed the House of Representatives, but so far is stalled by the U.S. Senate. Passage of the bill seems to have a slim chance, but just in case the Senators do find a way to attach this to other legislation, I include it here.

In the House bill, bankruptcy judges could reduce the principal balance of a homeowner's mortgage loan, lower the interest rate, and extend the terms.

The bill gives preference to lowering a homeowner's interest rate over cutting the principal balance. Also, if the balance is cut, the homeowner must share any profit from the eventual sale of the home.

Another provision of the bill is that before a homeowner seeks relief from a bankruptcy judge, she must show that she sought modification from her lender. If the lender offered to lower the homeowner's payments to 31 percent of the family's income and the homeowner refused that offer, she likely won't get additional help from a bankruptcy judge.

If you're planning to file for bankruptcy and your home is worth less than you owe the bank, you must contact your lender and try to work out a modification of the loan. If your lender says no, the bankruptcy judge will be able to consider a cramdown, if the new law passes before you file for bankruptcy.

Now that you understand the basics of how to use bankruptcy to save your home, let's take a closer look at what happens to other types of debt.

The Least You Need to Know

◆ You don't have to wait until your home goes into foreclosure to save your home using bankruptcy.

◆ Each state has its own homestead exemption rules that determine how much of your home's equity you can protect using bankruptcy.

◆ If you moved in the last 40 months, be sure you understand the special rules about homestead exemptions.

◆ A new bankruptcy law may make it easier to save your home if you owe more than it's worth.

Chapter

9

Getting a Fresh Financial Start

In This Chapter

- ◆ Debt types
- ◆ Chapter 7 discharges
- ◆ Chapter 13 discharges
- ◆ Debt not discharged

I'm sure you'd like to hear that all debts will disappear after you file for bankruptcy and that you can start from zero, but unfortunately, that's not the case. You will need to repay some debts if you want to keep an asset, such as your home or car. Others, such as alimony and child support, cannot be erased with any form of bankruptcy.

In this chapter, we look at what debts you can erase to get a fresh financial start, what debts you can restructure to make it easier for you to repay them, and what debts will remain after bankruptcy.

Secured vs. Unsecured Debt

First, I need to review secured versus unsecured debt. Secured debt is debt for which you put up collateral such as your house when you take a mortgage. If you don't make the mortgage payments, the bank can repossess your house. The same is true when you take a car loan.

There is also something called non-purchase-money secured debt. This is when the creditor does take a security interest, but does not provide the funding necessary to purchase the secured asset. In either Chapter 7 or Chapter 13 bankruptcy, your attorney may use Section 522 of the Bankruptcy Code to erase all or part of that security interest. Section 522 may likewise be used to erase all or part of a security interest created by a judgment against you.

Unsecured debt is debt that you agreed to by contract but did not put up any assets as collateral. The most common type of unsecured debt is credit card debt. Let's first take a look at all the types of unsecured debt that a Chapter 7 or Chapter 13 bankruptcy filing can erase:

- **Credit card debt**—This is the type of debt people most commonly want to erase by filing bankruptcy. Most will succeed with this goal if they complete the bankruptcy process, whether they choose to use Chapter 7 or Chapter 13. Unless a creditor can prove that you fraudulently completed an application or recently purchased a lot of luxury items, this debt will likely be erased when your bankruptcy is discharged.

- **Medical bills**—This is the primary reason many people end up in bankruptcy court. Your medical bills will be erased at the end of the bankruptcy process. Billions of dollars are discharged each year as part of a bankruptcy. I take a closer look at medical bills in Chapter 10.

- **Lawsuits**—If you've been sued and someone won a judgment against you in civil court, the person who won the judgment can try to collect by seizing your bank account, garnishing your wages, or putting a lien on your home. Luckily, most money judgments are almost always dischargeable in bankruptcy, regardless of the facts. Some regarding willful misconduct are not. I talk more about these shortly.

♦ **Leases and contracts**—If you have a lease or contract to sell real estate, buy a business, deliver merchandise, or fulfill any other obligation under that lease or contract, you can discharge your obligations and liabilities as part of a bankruptcy. But if the bankruptcy trustee thinks that the lease or contract can be sold to a third party to pay unsecured creditors or that you filed bankruptcy just to get rid of a particular contract agreement, he may not discharge the debt related to the lease or contract.

♦ **Personal loans or promissory notes**—If you borrowed money from the bank, a friend, or an associate without putting up an asset as collateral, that likely will be a personal loan or promissory note. You could have gotten this loan with a verbal agreement or just a handshake. The bankruptcy court will discharge this debt unless the creditor can prove that you obtained this debt fraudulently.

These are the most common unsecured debts that can be discharged as part of a bankruptcy. If you file for Chapter 13 bankruptcy, you may have to pay a portion of these debts as part of your repayment plan if you have a lot of discretionary income left over after paying your secured debts.

Debts Not Discharged by Chapter 7

Some debts cannot be discharged under any circumstances because a creditor successfully convinces the court that the debt should not be discharged. Some debts can be discharged if you convince the court that the debt fits within a narrow exception to the rule. Let's take a closer look at these debt discharge exceptions.

Debts Not Dischargeable for Any Reason

Some debts just can't be discharged for any reason. The most common of these are debts you owe for domestic support obligations. This includes alimony and child support. The domestic support obligation must have been established in …

- A separation agreement, divorce decree, or property settlement agreement.

- An order of the court.

- A determination by a child support enforcement agency that has the legal authority to impose support obligation.

Credit Cleaners _____

Although you can't discharge domestic support obligations as part of a Chapter 7 filing, you may be able to discharge some of the debt owed to a governmental child support collection agency using Chapter 13. If you owe child support, talk with your attorney about which bankruptcy to use.

Another major debt that cannot be discharged is money owed as fines, penalties, or restitution that was imposed upon you for violating a law. Some examples of these types of debt include the following:

- Fines or penalties for infractions, misdemeanors, or felonies

- Fines imposed because of contempt of court

- Fines imposed for violating governmental agency regulations

- Restitution you must pay to the victim of a crime in a federal criminal case

- Fines or penalties imposed under federal election law violations

Tax debts are another major category of debts that can't be discharged under Chapter 7 bankruptcy. Sometimes you can discharge tax liability if you meet all these conditions:

- You filed a tax return for the tax year or years in question.

- You filed that return for taxes due at least two years before you filed for bankruptcy.

- The taxes you owe were due at least three years before you filed for bankruptcy.

- You have not been assessed for your tax liability within 240 calendar days (eight months) before filing for bankruptcy. If you were in the middle of an offer to pay the taxes or filed for bankruptcy previously, the 240-day limit can be extended.

- The taxes were not incurred by you as an employer charged with the duty to withhold from your employees.

- You did not willfully evade the tax or file a fraudulent return.

> **Debt Dangers**
>
> If you pay taxes by borrowing money or using a credit card, the money you borrow will not be dischargeable under Chapter 7 bankruptcy. You can't turn a nondischargeable debt into a dischargeable debt by borrowing money to pay Uncle Sam.

Even if you meet all these requirements, your property may still be affected if the IRS or state taxing authority fixes a tax lien before your bankruptcy filing.

As you can see from these conditions, most people will not succeed in discharging taxes.

Even if you can prove these conditions exist, you will never be able to get *fraudulent income taxes* discharged. Property taxes also aren't dischargeable unless they became due more than a year before you filed for bankruptcy. Even if you can get property taxes discharged as part of a bankruptcy, a lien will remain on your property. You will have to pay off this lien if you want to transfer ownership of the property. For example, suppose you plan to sell the property: to get a clear title to complete the sale, you will have to pay off the lien.

> **def•i•ni•tion**
>
> **Fraudulent income taxes** include taxes due because you didn't file a return or taxes due because you intentionally avoided your tax obligations.

Other key debts that can't be discharged under Chapter 7 bankruptcy for any reason include the following:

◆ **Court fees**—You can't discharge fees imposed by a court for filing a case, a motion, a complaint, or an appeal.

◆ **Intoxicated driving debts**—If you kill or injure someone while driving illegally intoxicated by alcohol or drugs, any debts remaining from that incident cannot be discharged.

◆ **Condominium, cooperative, or homeowner's association fees**—You cannot discharge fees assessed after your bankruptcy filing date, but fees due before you file for bankruptcy can be discharged.

◆ **Debts for loans from a retirement plan**—You can't discharge debt for loans taken from an employer-sponsored retirement plan. But Chapter 13 does allow you to discharge this debt.

◆ **Debts you couldn't discharge in a previous bankruptcy**—If you filed an earlier bankruptcy case that was dismissed because of fraud or other bad acts, you cannot discharge debts that you tried to discharge in that earlier bankruptcy.

Creditor Objections to Discharge

Sometimes you'll ask for a debt to be discharged as part of a Chapter 7 bankruptcy that normally is discharged, but a creditor will object to that discharge. To stop a debt from being discharged, a creditor must …

◆ File a formal objection during your bankruptcy proceedings. This is called a complaint to determine dischargeablity.

◆ Prove that the debt was from intentionally fraudulent behavior, was from a false written statement about your financial condition, was from debts for luxuries, or was from recent cash advances.

◆ Prove that the debt was from a willful and malicious act.

◆ Prove that the debt was from embezzlement, larceny, or breach of fiduciary duty.

Even if creditors object, they may not be successful in trying to stop the discharge of the debt. Let's take a closer look at the types of debts for which a creditor can object to discharge.

Fraudulent Behavior

The bankruptcy court may see these acts as fraudulent behavior:

- You stopped payment on a check even though you kept the item you purchased.

- You wrote a check against insufficient funds even though you told the store owner, doctor, or other recipient that the check was good.

- You rented or borrowed an item that you used as collateral for a loan.

- You took a loan and promised to pay it back even though you had no intention to do so.

The creditor must prove that your fraudulent behavior was intentional, and he must have relied on that behavior to extend the credit.

False Written Statement

To prove that a debt should not be dischargeable if you offered a false written statement, the creditor must prove that …

- The false statement is written. Examples of acceptable written statements include a credit card application, a rental application, or a resumé.

- The false written statement must be a potentially significant factor in the creditor's decision to extend you the credit.

- The statement must relate to your financial condition or the financial condition of a business entity with which you are associated, or a person with whom you have a close relationship.

- The creditor relied on the statement.

- You intended to deceive the creditor.

Luxury Shopping Spree

The creditor can question your shopping spree only if you ran up more than $550 in debt to that creditor for luxury goods within the 90-day period before filing for bankruptcy. Any luxury charges will survive bankruptcy if the creditor successfully proves these last-minute charges. You will have to prove that your intent wasn't fraudulent.

Credit Cleaners

Luxury goods do not include things you need to support and maintain you and your family. The court will decide whether the goods you bought represent "reasonably necessary" expenses.

Cash Advances

If you get more than $825 in cash advances from one creditor within 70 days before filing for bankruptcy, the debt is not dischargeable. For the creditor to successfully challenge this debt discharge, the plan must be an open-ended consumer credit plan. There must be no date when the debt must be repaid. A credit card is an example of an open-ended consumer credit plan: you have no set date by which you must pay the debt, as long as you make monthly payments.

Debt Dangers

One of the worst things you can do is take a significant amount in cash advances on your credit cards, trying to prevent bankruptcy. If you do that in the 70 days before filing for bankruptcy, you may not be able to discharge the debt.

Willful and Malicious Acts

If you were involved in an act for which you intended to inflict injury to a person or his property, that could be considered a willful and malicious act. Examples of these types of acts include kidnapping; rape; arson; vandalism; deliberate cause of extreme anxiety, fear, or shock; and libel or slander. If someone has been awarded money for personal injury or property damage the debt will almost always be ruled nondischargeable, but the victim must object during your Chapter 7 bankruptcy case.

Embezzlement, Larceny, or Breach of Fiduciary Duty

A creditor to whom you owe a debt for *embezzlement*, *larceny*, or *breach of fiduciary duty* can successfully challenge the discharge of the debt.

def•i•ni•tion

Embezzlement involves taking property for which you have responsibility and using it for yourself.

Larceny is theft.

Breach of fiduciary duty means you have failed to live up to a duty of trust, such as one to manage property or money for someone.

Common examples of people who may have a fiduciary relationship include business partners, an attorney to a client, an estate executor to the beneficiary of the estate, a guardian to a ward, and a husband to his wife.

Discharge by Narrow Exception

You may be able to ask the bankruptcy judge for a special exception to discharge certain debts. Student loans are the most common debts that fall under this exception rule. If you want to discharge your student debt on the basis of "undue hardship," you must file a separate action with the court and obtain a court ruling in your favor. If you're not working with an attorney on your bankruptcy but you want to file for the special exception, you should hire an attorney to represent you on that motion.

To get an "undue hardship" ruling in your favor, three factors are considered:

 ◆ **Poverty**—You must prove that you cannot maintain a minimal living standard and repay the loan.

◆ **Hardship**—You must prove that your current financial condition will likely continue indefinitely. Someone who is elderly or disabled has the best chance to prove hardship.

◆ **Good faith**—You must prove that you made a good-faith effort to repay the debt. You probably won't pass this test if you file for bankruptcy soon after getting out of school or if you haven't looked extensively for employment.

As mentioned earlier, the other key type of debt that you may be able to get a judge to discharge is regular income taxes, provided that you meet the narrow conditions for a discharge.

Debts That Can Be Discharged Only by Chapter 13

Chapter 13 permits you to discharge some debts that can't be discharged under Chapter 7. Some key debts that can be discharged under Chapter 13 include these:

◆ Some child support. Chapter 7 doesn't allow you to discharge child support or alimony payments you owe to anyone, but Chapter 13 permits you to discharge at least some of your back child support owed to governmental child support collection agencies.

◆ Older income taxes (due more than three years before filing for bankruptcy). These taxes may be discharged as long as there's no evidence that you tried to avoid paying these taxes and as long as you filed an honest return. I talk more about the conditions for discharging taxes earlier.

◆ Marital debts other than alimony and child support.

◆ Debts incurred to pay a nondischargeable tax debt.

◆ Court fees.

◆ Condominium, cooperative, and homeowner's association fees.

- Debts for loans from a retirement plan.
- Debts that you couldn't discharge in a previous bankruptcy.

If you want to discharge any of these debts, you will need to file under Chapter 13 instead of Chapter 7.

Debts Not Discharged by Chapter 13

Many debts that can't be discharged under Chapter 7 also can't be discharged under Chapter 13. These include the following:

- Alimony and child support owed to an ex-spouse
- Criminal penalties (even money you owe on traffic tickets)
- Intoxicated driving debts
- Debts incurred for willful or malicious reasons
- Student loans (unless you can prove "hardship")
- Fraudulent debts

Debts and Creditors You Don't List

You could end up paying debts unnecessarily if you forget to list them on your bankruptcy papers. When you file those papers, you must list all of your creditors on your bankruptcy papers and provide their most current addresses. As long as you submitted a complete list, dischargeable debts will be discharged even if the creditor did not get an official notice of your bankruptcy.

But what happens if you forget to list a creditor? Or what if you didn't give the correct name or address for a creditor? When that happens, the creditor may not get an official notice and the debt may not be discharged.

But if you filed a Chapter 7 bankruptcy and it was a case without any assets to be distributed, the debt will be discharged unless it is a nondischargeable debt.

Since with a Chapter 7 bankruptcy the creditor could not have benefited from notice anyway (because no property was distributed), the court could discharge the debt. But because the lack of notice deprived the creditor of the opportunity to file a complaint in bankruptcy court and challenge the discharge, the debt could survive your bankruptcy if the creditor complains.

If a debtor shows up after your bankruptcy case is closed, you can reopen your case, name the creditor, and then seek an amended discharge. If it's the type of debt that would have been discharged anyway, the court may not allow you to reopen the case, since most creditors know that the debt is discharged anyway. If a creditor continues to try to collect a debt that would have been discharged, you can take the creditor to bankruptcy court on a contempt charge.

When you file a Chapter 13 bankruptcy, an error or omission in listing a debt can result in the debt still being due after discharge. Since with Chapter 13 the creditor may have gotten some repayment, all debts not listed in a Chapter 13 case generally survive the bankruptcy.

No matter what type of bankruptcy you file, always be sure to list all your debts. Take the time to request all your credit reports, and make sure you have the names and addresses for all creditors that show on that report. List all medical bills. Remember, most times when you go to a hospital, even if it's a few hours in the emergency room, you could get bills from several doctors, radiology, and other services.

Also check to see if anyone has placed liens against any of your properties. Take the extra time to be sure you're not missing any debtors so you can avoid one of the biggest mistakes you can make: forgetting to list a creditor. I talk more about putting together a list of your debts in Chapter 2.

Now that we've taken a look at debts, let's focus on medical debt and how bankruptcy can help ease your worries so you can take the time you need to get well.

The Least You Need to Know

◆ Most unsecured debt can be erased when you complete the bankruptcy process.

◆ You must continue making payments on secured debt if you want to keep an asset, such as your house or car.

◆ Some debts are dischargeable in Chapter 13 bankruptcy but are not dischargeable in a Chapter 7 bankruptcy, so review your debts carefully with your attorney when choosing the type of bankruptcy.

◆ Make sure you list all your debts. If you forget to list a debt, the debt could survive after your bankruptcy process is complete.

Chapter  10

Clearing Out Medical Debt

In This Chapter

- ◆ Erasing medical bills
- ◆ Keeping medical debt unsecured
- ◆ The disability factor
- ◆ Seeking help
- ◆ Erasing debt

If you filed bankruptcy because of mounting medical debt, you're not alone. Illness and medical bills cause half of all bankruptcies—and with 45 million people uninsured in this country, one can only expect these numbers to climb.

In fact, a study by Harvard University showed that even those with health insurance are not immune from needing to file bankruptcy if struck with a serious illness. Often during a serious illness, people lose their job and, along with it, their health insurance.

In this chapter, I look at how to deal with medical bills before and during a bankruptcy filing. I discuss the importance of keeping medical bills an unsecured debt. I also look at how disability may strengthen your case for bankruptcy relief. Finally, I give you options for finding help in treating your medical illness during and after a bankruptcy filing.

Why People Seek Bankruptcy Protection for Medical Bills

People don't necessarily have thousands of dollars in medical bills when they seek bankruptcy. In fact, research shows about 20 percent of bankruptcy filings involve a medical debt of less than $1,000; about 40 percent involve a medical debt of less than $5,000; and 13 percent of bankruptcy filings involve a medical debt of over $10,000. In all these cases, there could be medical expenses charged on credit cards as well.

With 60 percent of bankruptcy filers carrying debt below $5,000, you may wonder why people didn't try to make some sort of payment arrangements with their health-care provider to pay off the debt rather than file bankruptcy. That's because the medical industry seeks help from professional debt collectors more quickly each year.

The medical collection industry is inflexible and often will not work out reasonable payment plans for those who cannot pay off the debt quickly. You'll find hospitals, doctors, and medical collection agencies rush to the courthouse to file small-claims lawsuits (those less than $5,000) when a person is just 90 days late on a bill. That way they can attempt to get their money by garnishing wages once they get a court order. People are forced to file bankruptcy to stop the garnishments.

Small-claims courts in some areas of the country are clogged with such suits, with medical debt lawsuits making up a large portion of a court's docket. And this trend is increasing as many hospitals, doctors, and other medical-related businesses turn their delinquent accounts over to collection agencies in 30 or 60 days rather than waiting the traditional 150 days before doing so. Another trend is for medical-related businesses to sue in small-claims court for very trivial amounts, say $100, rather than just write the debt off as a bad debt.

With unemployment nearly 10 percent in 2009 and many people losing health insurance, the number of people unable to pay for needed medical care likely will go up. The problem will only get worse.

If you do get sued by a health-care provider or collection agency, they may try to get you to sign a repayment plan to drop the suit. Don't sign a repayment agreement that you cannot afford to pay and then default on it. If you do sign an agreement, make sure that the agreement you sign does not include a clause where you waive your right to have your income and property claimed exempt from creditors. Most states do allow you to declare your home, and in some cases your income, exempt from creditors.

For example, if you can only afford $15 a month, then tell the judge this when you get to court. You should be ready to prove your income levels by bringing detailed information about income and living expenses—such as utility bills, rent or mortgage, grocery receipts—to court with you.

You may wonder what property is exempt from creditors and debt collectors in your state. Almost all states exempt income under a certain amount to protect those with low incomes from creditors. For example, your state might have legislation on the books that says a creditor can only seize any net income over $250 per week. If you make $250 or less per week, your income is exempt. Your state might put a cap on how much of your wages can be garnished, perhaps no more than 15 percent. Sit down with an attorney to review your options. Often you can get an initial one-hour consultation at no or little cost.

In addition, your state might have declared that government benefits—such as Social Security, welfare, unemployment compensation, and veteran's benefits—might also be completely or partially exempt. Your state might also have exempted retirement benefits (pensions), child support, worker's compensation, life insurance policies, and personal injury awards. The cash you have in the bank might be protected, as are your car and other assets, such as your clothing, furniture, work tools, and a vehicle.

Don't just accept whatever a collector tells you as the truth. You may have more protection than you think.

Medical Bills

One of your biggest problems before filing for bankruptcy will be making sure you don't miss any of your outstanding bills. You must list all your creditors when you file. If you miss a creditor, the debt could survive the bankruptcy.

You may find it difficult to pull together a list of all the medical providers you owe for medical expenses because they don't usually report past-due bills to a credit bureau. Therefore, you can't rely on just your credit report to build an accurate list. You may not even get a bill for months after a hospital visit.

Basically, you have two different types of bills: those for treatment and those for medication. Let's look at how these are usually handled and how you'll end up dealing with the debt.

Treatment Bills

As long as you get all your treatment through one doctor's office or one clinic, your treatment bills may be easy to track. But one-stop shopping for medical care is not the norm. Usually people go to one doctor for primary care and then numerous specialists, depending on the necessary treatment.

Things get even more complicated if you need treatment in a hospital. The last time my husband went to a hospital emergency room, we got a bill from the emergency room doctor, the radiologist who read the x-rays, the laboratory, and the hospital. If a specialist had been called in, we'd have had a bill from that doctor as well. Some bills didn't even show up at our doorstep for two months. That's common anytime you go to a hospital.

If you paid your bill by credit card, you don't have to list the doctor separately. You owe the money to the credit card company, not the doctor. Just be sure you list all the credit card companies you owe.

Credit Cleaners _____

> When filing for bankruptcy, be sure you've accounted for all possible bills. You may want to call the hospital billing office to see if you can get a list of all doctor's groups that could possibly bill you. Then check your list of doctors and be sure you've included them on your creditors list.

Medication

Most people pay for medication by using their credit cards, so you probably won't have separate bills for medication. You will just need to include all your credit card companies as creditors.

But some people need to take medication intravenously and could get separate medical billing for that. If you go to a doctor's office or a clinic to get your medication, be sure to include any billing from them in your list of creditors.

Unsecured Debt

Remember, medical debt is unsecured debt. You haven't put your house up as collateral to get the medical services. Don't make the mistake of turning that into secured debt by taking out an equity line against your home to pay your medical bills.

An equity line works just like any other mortgage debt. If you can't make the payments, the bank can foreclose on your home and you will lose the property.

Debt Dangers _____

> Keep medical debt unsecured by using credit cards, not an equity line or other loan tied to an asset. Since all medical debt is unsecured, why risk losing your home?

Dealing With Disability

If you've become disabled by your illness, you may be able to use that disability to get "hardship" status with some of your debts. You may find that you can get a loan modification on your mortgage, or you may be able to erase your student loan.

Although I don't wish disability on anyone, if you do become disabled, talk with your attorney. You might be able to renegotiate terms on secured debt and erase debts that you might otherwise not be able to erase with a bankruptcy.

Timing and Choice of Bankruptcy

Timing your bankruptcy, as well as the type of bankruptcy you choose to file, can be critical when medical bills are involved. If you incur medical bills after you file a Chapter 7 or while you are in a Chapter 13 bankruptcy case, you are responsible and liable for paying those medical bills. But if you incur medical bills while you are in a Chapter 13 case and then convert to Chapter 7, those medical bills are dischargeable.

Debt Dangers

If any of your medical debt includes a doctor bill, you likely will have to find a new doctor. Your doctor could refuse to treat you in the future if you file for bankruptcy.

So if you are in the middle of an expensive treatment plan, be sure your bankruptcy attorney understands your current medical expenses and whether or not they will continue to build after you file bankruptcy. If you file a Chapter 7 bankruptcy, you won't be able to file bankruptcy again for eight years.

Seeking Outside Help

You may be concerned about how to pay for continuing medical needs after filing for bankruptcy. Help is out there for people with many different kinds of diseases, even if they don't have any way to pay for care.

If you're worried about paying for medication, talk with both your doctor and your pharmacist. Most pharmaceutical companies offer assistance to people who cannot afford their drugs. Your doctor may also get free samples and be able to help you.

If you've listed your doctor as one the creditors who won't be paid, you may not be able to seek help from him. Instead, you'll need to contact your county's health clinics for treatment after a bankruptcy filing. Most county health clinics determine their fees based on a sliding scale.

Medicaid

If you can't afford medical care, you may qualify for Medicaid. You will need to jump through a lot of hoops, but if you qualify that could reduce a lot of anxiety, especially if you've been disabled by your illness. Call your state's health department to discuss the eligibility requirements.

Here are the key categories of eligible groups:

- Families who meet their state's Aid to Families with Dependent Children.
- Pregnant women and children under age 6 whose family income is at or below 133 percent of the federal poverty level.
- Children ages 6 to 19 with family income up to 100 percent of the federal poverty level. In some states there could be a higher threshold.
- Caretakers (relatives or guardians), who take care of children under age 18 (or 19 if still in high school).

- Supplemental Security Income (SSI) recipients or in some states aged, blind, or disabled people who meet requirements that are more restrictive than SSI.

- Individuals and couples who are living in medical institutions and who have monthly income up to 300 percent of the SSI income standard.

In addition to these categories, people who don't meet the strict income guidelines may qualify under medically needy. These include people who have too much money or resources like savings to be eligible categorically. Not all states have a medically needy program, but some states do provide assistance to the following:

Credit Cleaners

Thirty-five states do offer some or all of these group benefits in the medically needy category, so if you do need help, don't hesitate to call your state's health department to find out if you are eligible for help with your medical needs.

- Children under age 21 who are full-time students

- Aged persons (age 65 and older)

- Blind persons

- Disabled persons

Medicaid Services

If you do qualify for Medicaid, you will be entitled to medical care that includes:

- Inpatient hospital

- Outpatient hospital (in rural areas, this could include health clinics)

- Laboratory and x-ray

- Certified pediatric and family nurse practitioners

- Nursing facility services

- Family planning services and supplies

- ◆ Medical and surgical dentist services

- ◆ Some home health services

- ◆ Nurse midwife services

- ◆ Pregnancy-related services and services for other conditions that might complicate pregnancy

- ◆ 60-day postpartum pregnancy–related services

States also have the option to offer additional services, so if your doctor recommends a treatment not on the list, check with your Medicaid counselor to see if coverage is possible.

While you may find you have to wait longer for medical care than you did prior to getting help from Medicaid, you won't have to worry about mounting medical bills. Also, don't get frustrated with the paperwork; it will be worth it in the end to get the medical care you need without having to worry about mounting medical debt.

State Children's Health Insurance Program

In addition to Medicaid, states have a health insurance program for children up to age 19 called the State Children's Health Insurance Program (SCHIP). In some states, SCHIP is part of the state's Medicaid program; in others, it's separate. Some states combine both types of programs to provide the most comprehensive coverage for children.

SCHIP programs are for parents who have too much money to be eligible for Medicaid but not enough to buy private insurance. Most states offer this insurance to families with children whose income level is at or below 200 percent of the federal poverty level. Each state has its own income eligibility rules, so you will need to call your state's health department to determine your family's eligibility.

Credit Cleaners

Census Bureau data is used to determine the federal poverty level based on the size of the household. You can find out the federal poverty level for your family size at www.census.gov/hhes/www/poverty/threshld/thresh08.html.

Some charities will also help people with certain conditions. These charities include Caring Voice Coalition, Chronic Disease Fund, The HealthWell Foundation, National Marrow Patient Assistance Program, National Organization for Rare Disorders, and Patient Advocate Foundation's Co-Pay Relief. Following is a brief summary of the types of support each provides.

Caring Voice Coalition

The coalition can help you with the cost of some of your prescriptions if you have one of the following conditions: pulmonary arterial hypertension, idiopathic pulmonary fibrosis, alpha-1 antitrypsin deficiency, chronic granulomatus, or Huntington's disease. You can find out more at www.caringvoice.org or by calling 1-888-267-1440.

Chronic Disease Fund

This fund offers two types of assistance. One program, Patient Financial Assistance, provides copay assistance for certain drugs (as long as your drug plan covers the drug) if you cannot afford the copay. It also offers a Free Drug Program to people who meet income, asset, and medical condition guidelines.

Help covers these conditions: age-related macular degeneration, alcohol dependence, ankylosing spondylitis, asthma, breast cancer, colorectal cancer, growth hormone deficiency, multiple myeloma, multiple sclerosis, myelodysplastic syndrome, non-small-cell lung cancer, and psoriasis.

You can find more information at www.cdfund.org or by calling 1-877-968-7233.

The HealthWell Foundation

This foundation will help you pay your drug copays if you have insurance, or help you pay your monthly premiums if you are eligible but can't afford to pay for insurance. You must meet income criteria to qualify for help. Income criteria is based on multiples of the poverty level.

Diseases the foundation supports include acute porphyries, age-related macular degeneration, anemia associated with chronic renal insufficiency or chronic renal failure, ankylosing spondylitis, asthma, breast cancer, carcinoid tumors, chemotherapy-induced anemia or nutropenia, colorectal carcinoma, cutaneous T-cell lymphoma, head and neck cancer, Hodgkin's disease, idiopathic thrombocytopenic purpura, immunosuppressive treatment for solid organ transplant recipients, iron overload as a result of blood transfusions, non-Hodgkin's lymphoma, non-small-cell lung cancer, psoriasis, psoriatic arthritis, rheumatoid arthritis, secondary hyperparathyroidism, and Wilms' tumor.

You can find out more at www.healthwellfoundation.org or by calling 1-800-675-8416.

National Marrow Patient Assistance Program and Financial Assistance Fund

This program provides assistance for the cost of prescription drugs that must be taken as part of recovery after a marrow transplant. To qualify, you must have used the National Marrow Patient Assistance Program's donor registry to find your marrow transplant donor. The donor also must not be a family member.

You can find out more about this program at www.marrow.org or by calling 1-888-999-6743.

National Organization for Rare Disorders

This organization can help you obtain prescriptions that you can't afford or help pay for drugs not yet on the market. The organization's database includes more than 1,000 diseases.

To see which diseases this program includes, or to learn more about the organization, go to www.rarediseases.org or call 203-744-0100. You can leave a voicemail message at 1-800-999-6673.

Patient Advocate Foundation's Co-Pay Relief

This foundation will pay your full copay for prescriptions that your insurance covers, as long as you take them to treat a medical condition of interest to the foundation. Eligible conditions include breast, lung, prostate, kidney, colon, pancreatic, and head/neck cancers; malignant brain tumors; lymphoma; sarcoma; diabetes; multiple myeloma; myelodsyplastic syndrome (and other pre-leukemia diseases); osteoporosis; selected autoimmune disorders; and secondary issues as a result of chemotherapy treatment.

You can find more information about this foundation at www.copays. org or by calling 1-866-512-3861.

You can see that there is a lot of help out there for people with serious medical conditions, so don't skip seeking medical treatment just because you filed for bankruptcy.

Discharging Your Debt So You Can Focus on Healing

Filing bankruptcy to discharge medical debt so you can focus on healing is a wise choice. But before doing so, talk with your attorney about future medical needs. You may want to delay a bankruptcy filing to finish the treatment program you're currently on. Your attorney can help advise you on the best timing for your bankruptcy based on your current medical needs.

If the bank is ready to foreclose on your home, you may have no choice but to file for bankruptcy if you want to stall the foreclosure. But you do need to be realistic. Can you still afford to make the mortgage payments on that home once your medical debt is erased? Even if you file for bankruptcy, if you can't make the payments on a secured debt like a mortgage, you will likely lose your home.

Now that we've taken a closer look at medical care and bankruptcy, let's focus on divorce and its impact on filing for bankruptcy.

The Least You Need to Know

◆ Medical debt is unsecured. Don't pay for it using a loan for which you've put up collateral, such as an equity line.

◆ You can erase all medical debt, as long as you've listed all your creditors. Make sure you don't leave out any doctors, laboratories, or clinics.

◆ Just because you filed bankruptcy doesn't mean you won't be able to get the care you need. Government and private agencies are there to help.

◆ If you can't afford medical care, don't hesitate to seek out government health-care programs like Medicaid and SCHIP to get help paying for medical care.

Chapter **11**

Cleaning Up a Financial Mess After Divorce

In This Chapter

- ◆ Debt division
- ◆ Ex-spouses and debt
- ◆ Credit cleaning

Divorce can be an expensive process, and the financial mess left after a divorce can be a serious drain on anyone's finances. Often at least one spouse files for bankruptcy to clear out debt remaining from the marriage. Even if your partner took responsibility for the debt, you could end up having to pay off the debt if he or she files for bankruptcy.

In this chapter, I take a closer look at marital debts and talk about the differences between joint debt and individual debt, and how it impacts ex-spouses. Finally, I discuss what you need to do to clear out those bad financial memories.

Dividing Debt—Joint Debt vs. Individual Debt

You and your spouse may make an agreement about how you want to split up the debt in a divorce agreement, but that doesn't mean the law will see it that way. More important, it's not necessarily how your creditors will view it.

For example, suppose you and your husband bought a car together. In your divorce agreement, you decide that your spouse will take the car and assume the car payments. Suppose that, six months after the divorce, your ex-spouse stops making payments on the car and it gets repossessed.

If you have no contact with your ex-spouse, your first notice that he stopped making payments could be when you get a collection notice from the creditor. Even though he took responsibility for the debt, unless he refinanced the car, you're still a joint debtor on that loan and you could be stuck paying it off or filing bankruptcy to get rid of the debt.

In fact, you could be stuck paying any of your ex's debt on which you signed jointly while you were married. This includes credit card agreements. As soon as you think you may be facing divorce or separation, you should alert your creditors and close any joint accounts so that your soon-to-be-ex can't charge a lot of stuff and stick you with the bill.

By law, a creditor cannot close a joint account because of a change in marital status, but can do so at the request of either spouse. You should make sure the request is made as soon as possible using these steps:

- ◆ Notify your creditor in writing that you and your spouse plan to separate. Indicate that you will no longer be responsible for charges on that account as of a specific date and ask that the account be frozen.

◆ Send the letter by certified mail return receipt requested so you have proof of the date it was sent and the date it was received by your creditor.

◆ Verify the account has been frozen.

Credit Cleaners _____

Don't leave anything to chance. Be sure to put in writing all conversations you may have with your creditors about a pending separation or divorce. Send the correspondence by certified mail return receipt requested to be sure you have proof you notified your creditors about a change in marital status.

By law, a creditor has no obligation to change joint accounts to individual accounts. You will likely be required to reapply for credit on an individual basis. Your application can be denied. That's why I recommend that every individual, whether married or single, maintain at least one credit card in his or her own name without his or her spouse on the card.

Joint debt on secured assets, such as a mortgage or car, can be much more difficult to split. If you have a mortgage or home equity loan, the lender is likely to require refinancing to remove someone from that obligation.

In today's world, many couples need two salaries to qualify for a mortgage loan, so if that's the case for you and your spouse, in order to truly get off the mortgage you may need to decide to sell the property.

In 2009 and 2010, that could be a difficult choice because so many homes are underwater. You may need to come up with cash at closing. Talk with your attorney about the best options. One option to consider may be a short sale, where you find a buyer that will buy the home for less than the mortgage. Your lender would have to agree to the terms of the short sale. Be sure your attorney protects your credit rating as best as possible during the negotiation.

Another option is to give the home to the bank by a deed in lieu of foreclosure. Yes, your credit rating will take a hit, but it won't be as bad as having a foreclosure on your record. A foreclosure costs a bank $50,000 or more. In exchange for avoiding that cost, banks will usually work out some wording for your credit report that will not be as bad as a foreclosure. But work with a real estate attorney to be sure you are getting the best deal possible.

Joint Account vs. Authorized User

One key distinction you need to make is whether the credit accounts you have with your soon-to-be ex-spouse are joint accounts or individual accounts with your spouse as an authorized user. You should handle these two types of accounts differently.

A joint account is one in which your income and the income of your spouse, financial assets, and credit history were used to apply for the account. Even if you handle paying the bills on your spouse's individual accounts, only the person whose name is on the application will be held responsible by the creditor. If you have a joint account, your creditor will report credit history of a joint account to credit bureaus using both names if the account was opened after June 1, 1977. Both of you will be held responsible for outstanding bills.

The key advantage of using both incomes is that you make a stronger case to a creditor who is granting a loan or credit card. You likely will end up with a higher credit limit. But when two people apply for credit together, each is responsible for the debt. This is true even if a divorce decree assigns separate debt obligations to each spouse. Former spouses who run up bills and don't pay them can hurt their ex-partner's credit histories on jointly held accounts.

If you open an individual account, you may authorize your spouse to use it, but you control the usage of the account. If your spouse is a joint user but did not apply jointly, you can ask to have his or her name removed from the list of authorized people if you plan to separate or divorce.

Be sure to do this in writing as soon as you know there is a possibility of separation or divorce. Send the letter by certified mail so you have proof of the date you sent the letter and ask for a return receipt so you have proof that the company received your letter.

If you name your spouse as an authorized user, a creditor who reports the credit history to a credit bureau must report it in your spouse's name as well as in yours if the account was opened after June 1, 1977. So if your ex's name is still on your credit card as an authorized user, not only can he or she continue to charge on that account, your credit reports will remain linked.

The big disadvantage to adding someone as an authorized user is that they have no obligation to pay the bills on items they charge.

A husband and wife are much better off having primarily individual cards. If they do need one card for major purchases, they may decide to apply for a joint account, but use that card sparingly. While you don't want to plan for divorce throughout a marriage, you do need to protect yourself—especially if your spouse tends to be a big spender.

If you do divorce or separate, pay special attention to the status of your credit accounts. If you maintain joint accounts during this time, it's important to make regular payments so your credit reports won't suffer, even if it means you get stuck with most of the debt. As long as there's an outstanding balance on a joint account, you and your spouse are responsible for it.

When I divorced after my first marriage, I didn't think my first husband was very responsible about paying bills. I was the one who paid all the bills. To avoid a major credit problem, I took the responsibility to pay the remaining balances on credit cards. In exchange for that responsibility, I was granted the savings accounts, which covered most of the outstanding debt.

Debt Dangers

You need to think about how your ex paid bills and who is the most responsible party. If you believe you are this person and you will leave the marriage with joint debts, negotiate the best deal you can on those debts, but be the one in control of what happens to the payoff of those debts.

Community Property vs. Common-Law Property

What happens to the debts if one spouse files for bankruptcy depends on the laws in the state where you live. Marital debts are handled differently in states with community property rules than those with common-law property rules.

Community Property States

Nine states have community property rules: Arizona, California, Idaho, Louisiana, Nevada, New Mexico, Texas, Washington, and Wisconsin. Couples in Alaska can elect to have their property treated as community property if they sign an agreement to that effect.

In community property states, any debts incurred by either spouse during a marriage, even if a spouse signs a debt agreement without the other spouse knowing about it, are considered "community debts." Any debts incurred before the marriage or after the separation or divorce are considered separate debts.

In community property states, when a bankruptcy is filed, all community debts can be subject to discharge even if only one spouse files. This means the nonfiling spouse can benefit from the other spouse's decision to file bankruptcy.

So if you are in a community property state and bankruptcy is being contemplated before a divorce, one spouse can decide to take the hit to his or her credit history and leave the other spouse's record clear of a bankruptcy.

This strategy works only if one spouse has no separate debt. The other spouse with both separate debt and "community debts" would be the likely person to file for bankruptcy to wipe the slate clean.

 Credit Cleaners _____

> If you're contemplating both bankruptcy and divorce and you have a lot of marital debt, talk with your attorney about how debt will be handled in a bankruptcy. Depending on the laws of your state, the timing of the bankruptcy could be critical to being certain all your debt will be discharged.

If all debt is community debt, a divorcing spouse won't likely get the soon-to-be ex to file bankruptcy and destroy his or her credit. That type of agreement likely will work only if the spouse who agrees to destroy his or her credit also has a lot of separate debt to discharge.

Common-Law Property States

The rest of the states are common-law property states. In these states, either spouse who incurs debt before getting married is considered to be taking separate debt. Debts incurred during the marriage could be either separate or joint debt.

If you take debt jointly by opening a joint account, or if the creditor considered credit information from both spouses in making the loan, the debt is considered joint debt. Even if only one spouse took the loan, if the debt was for necessary items, such as food, clothing, and child-care expenses, the debt could be considered a joint debt.

Any debt that does not meet the criteria mentioned previously is handled as a separate debt in a bankruptcy filing. So if only one spouse files for bankruptcy, the bankruptcy can impact the joint debts and that spouse's individual debt. The other spouse's separate debts are unaffected even if they were incurred during marriage.

Common-Law Marriages

What if you never got married? Bankruptcy will impact your joint debts differently, depending upon whether or not you live in a state that recognizes common-law marriages.

Only a handful of states recognize marriage of heterosexual couples even if the couple never got a marriage license or had a marriage ceremony. This type of marriage is called a common-law marriage. Contrary to popular belief, you don't just qualify for a common-law marriage because you lived together for a certain number of years. In order to have a valid common-law marriage, you must do all of the following:

◆ Live together for a significant period of time (not defined in any state).

◆ Hold yourselves as a married couple—typically this means using the same last name, referring to the other as "my husband" or "my wife," and filing a joint tax return.

◆ Intend to get married eventually.

When a common-law marriage exists, the spouses receive the same legal treatment given to formally married couples, including the requirement that they go through a legal divorce to end the marriage.

Common-law marriage is recognized only in the following states:

◆ Alabama

◆ Colorado

◆ District of Columbia

◆ Georgia (if created before 1/1/97)

◆ Idaho (if created before 1/1/96)

◆ Iowa

◆ Kansas

◆ Montana

◆ New Hampshire (for inheritance purposes only)

◆ Ohio (if created before 10/10/91)

◆ Oklahoma

◆ Pennsylvania (if created before 1/1/05)

◆ Rhode Island

◆ South Carolina

◆ Texas

◆ Utah

If you live in one of the states that recognize common-law marriages, seek legal advice if you plan to separate and have joint debts. You don't want to have any surprises six months to a year later if your ex files bankruptcy and sticks you with all the unpaid bills.

Impact on Ex-Spouses

One of the worst things you can find out is that an ex-spouse filed for bankruptcy separately after the divorce. Creditors on any joint debt that he or she was responsible for paying can come chasing after you. As long as your name is on the joint debt, the creditor won't likely accept the divorce decree debt separation agreement.

Debt Dangers

If you had a lot of joint credit cards and your ex-spouse is taking responsibility for them, be sure that the debt is consolidated into a personal loan in his or her name. Leaving the debt on the credit card with his or her agreement to pay won't help you if bankruptcy is filed in the future. The creditor can go after you for the money even if your spouse agreed to pay the debt.

The only way to protect yourself is to be sure that all debt left from a marriage is separated legally. For example, if your ex-spouse will be responsible for paying a car loan or home mortgage, he or she needs to refinance the debt separately.

Unfortunately, if the debt involves a major purchase, it may be difficult for one spouse to have enough income to refinance the debt. In this case, you may want to sell the asset and split any profits.

Clearing Out Bad Financial Memories

When the divorce is finalized, it's critical that you take a look at all your credit reports and be certain that your credit information is accurate. In Chapter 13, I talk about how to do credit repair. If debts have been legally separated, be sure the old debt is shown as paid off or no longer your responsibility.

Credit-reporting agencies tend to be slow about updating records. They depend on the creditor reporting changes to an account. If a creditor was supposed to make changes and did not, write to the credit bureau telling them about the needed change. Send whatever documentation you have to prove the change should be made.

Credit Cleaners

Don't wait for your creditors to report changes to your debt status. Check your credit report and ask that needed changes be made. The faster you clean up your credit report, the sooner your credit score will improve.

The credit-reporting agencies will contact your creditor to verify the information. Unfortunately, the credit-reporting agencies tend to believe the creditor over you, so be sure you send proof of your claim in writing.

After one divorce, my ex-spouse and I had to split two homes. We had a townhouse that was an investment property and a home where we lived. I took the townhouse because I could more easily afford the payments, and my ex-spouse took the home. He planned to sell it but could afford the payments until it sold. We planned to split any profits from the sale of the home. The townhouse had no profit at the time of the divorce, so that was signed over to me free and clear.

I continued to make all the payments on time on the townhouse, but my ex decided to stop making payments on the house when it didn't sell quickly and moved out. I didn't even know the house was at risk of foreclosure until I received a notice in the mail.

I ended up working with a real estate agent and getting the home sold as a short sale. My ex-spouse had damaged the home in anger after the divorce.

Unfortunately, this mess stayed on my credit history for seven years, even though my ex was responsible based on the divorce decree. When I sent a note to the credit-reporting agencies with a copy of the decree, all they would do is put a note on my credit file that I disputed the debt history on the home payments.

Payments were always on time while we were married. Luckily, I kept proof of on-time payments in my files, because they came in handy when I applied for a new mortgage before the negative mark fell off my credit report.

I was able to get a mortgage even with the black mark because I was up front with the mortgage broker when I applied for a new mortgage. I showed the mortgage broker the divorce decree. He explained that when we submitted the mortgage package to the underwriter, we would need to explain the black mark with a letter and include a copy of the divorce decree. I also attached documentation showing that I had made on-time payments before the divorce.

So even if you end up with a black mark because an ex-spouse stops paying a debt, it's not the end of the world. Just be sure you have the proof that it was a debt for which your ex-spouse took responsibility.

Creditors are accustomed to seeing a financial mess after a divorce, but be ready to make the case that you will be an on-time payer if you take on a new loan. The best way to do that is to have several years of payment coupons that show you paid on time.

You should keep your debt-payment records for at least three years, but I recommend that you keep mortgage payments for the life of the loan, just in case the bank makes an error in recording a payment. This can become a critical issue when you near the end of the term of a loan or want to pay off the loan early. Errors in recording payments do occur, and if you don't have written proof that you made the payment, you won't have a leg to stand on.

 Credit Cleaners

The faster you work on cleaning up your debt history after a divorce, the better. If you do need to file bankruptcy, remember that this could impact your ex-spouse if you have joint debts. You may not care if you negatively impact your ex-spouse, but if you did take responsibility for a debt, you should at least notify him or her of your intent to file bankruptcy.

In fact, if your marriage is ending because of money problems, talk with your divorce attorneys about the possibility of filing for bankruptcy jointly. That might be your best bet for cleaning up debt problems so neither of you faces a financial shock after the divorce.

While you might hate your ex and never want to be in the same room with him or her again, a joint Chapter 7 filing may entail only a few minutes of unrelieved grimacing at the meeting of creditors. Even apart from sidestepping domestic dischargeability issues, the joint filing will cut filing fees in half and lawyer's fees nearly in half.

If you wait until after the divorce, you would each have to hire your own bankruptcy attorney, and you each would have to pay filing fees. You can save hundreds of dollars by biting the bullet and filing bankruptcy jointly.

I would not recommend that you consider filing Chapter 13 bankruptcy, because that would mean that you would be tied to your ex for three to five years in order to work through a repayment plan. You must be ready to file for Chapter 7, even if that means you might lose some assets you otherwise would keep.

In most states, you won't lose your house unless you have too much equity in that house. But if you do have that much equity in the house, selling the home could be your best bet to separate your finances and avoid bankruptcy.

Now that we've looked at the mess divorce can make of your credit reports, let's take a closer look at how you can clean up a credit report mess.

The Least You Need to Know

♦ When filing for divorce, don't only divide debt responsibilities; be sure your name is off any debt your ex-spouse agrees to pay.

♦ If your ex-spouse files bankruptcy and gets a debt discharged on which you are a joint debtor, you could get stuck paying the debt.

◆ After a divorce, be certain your debt is accurately separated on your credit reports.

◆ Consider filing for Chapter 7 bankruptcy to clean up a credit mess before your divorce.

Part 4

Life After Bankruptcy

In this part, you'll discover the basics about how to repair your credit history after bankruptcy, delve into job issues that you may face when you file bankruptcy, and explore how you can restart your credit life after bankruptcy. If you're married and only one of you filed for bankruptcy, you'll learn how to manage your financial life to minimize the impact of bankruptcy on your ability to get credit.

Chapter 12

Managing Your Money After Bankruptcy

In This Chapter

- ◆ Accepting responsibility
- ◆ Making it a family project
- ◆ Drafting a budget
- ◆ Removing temptation
- ◆ Watching for trouble signs

Before your bankruptcy can be discharged, you're required to take a money-management course. You can do this in the classroom or online, and it takes only two hours. That's handy for fulfilling the requirement, but it really isn't enough time to help you make the life changes you need to be able to avoid bankruptcy in the future.

In this chapter, I review some key money-management issues that likely contributed to your filing for bankruptcy in the first place. Then I explore how you can make changes and manage your money to avoid this type of financial crisis again.

Taking Responsibility for Your Spending Habits

You definitely want to avoid getting caught up in the same financial mess you did before filing for bankruptcy. Deal with any issues of compulsive spending that may have driven you to bankruptcy in the first place. I discuss shortly how to develop a budget and stick to it, but before you can even go there, you need to change some bad spending habits.

Credit Cleaners

If you think compulsive spending drove you to bankruptcy, think about joining Debtors Anonymous (www.debtorsanonymous. com) for support. They offer support groups online to help you get control of your spending.

- Don't buy anything you can't pay for when you get your next credit card bill. In fact, don't even carry a credit card with you when you go shopping. If you see something you think you need, go home, sleep on the decision overnight, and see if you still want it in the morning.

- Get into the habit of paying your credit cards in full each month. Don't think of your credit cards as a way to pay for things over time. Think of them more as a way to avoid carrying cash. But do keep a running tally of how much you charge each month so you don't exceed what you can afford to pay with your monthly paycheck.

Get Family Support

You can't make a change in your spending patterns without getting the full support and cooperation of your family. Even if you decide to change and get control of your spending habits, you'll fail if your spouse and kids don't agree.

Sit down and have a family meeting about the new reality, and set rules that all will agree to live by before spending. Many families set a dollar amount for miscellaneous spending—for example, $50—that can be spent without a family meeting. But when the dollar amount will be exceeded or the purchase falls outside the budget, there must be a family discussion before the money is spent.

You'll all have to make trade-offs. For example, suppose your wife decides that your daughter needs a new winter coat that costs $100. There isn't enough money in the budget for that new coat. You'll need to decide what spending can be put off in the budget so your daughter can buy the coat. After discussing what needs to be given up, your daughter might decide she doesn't need a new coat after all.

Set a standing rule that a purchase cannot be made unless the cash is on hand to pay for it. Don't get into the habit of paying for things on money due to come in—unless, of course, it's your regular paycheck. Too many times, people expect a bonus or other cash infusion that never comes or comes in

> **Debt Dangers**
>
> You can't get control of spending in a vacuum. You need the support of all members in your family. Otherwise, the actions of your family will negate any changes you make.

at a lower amount than expected. That's happening often today since the downturn in the economy in 2008. Bonuses have been cut, as has overtime pay.

Job losses continue to mount, so don't count your cash until it actually comes in the door. Even better, as you build your budget, set aside some cash for emergency situations so you'll have money that you need without taking on credit.

Now let's take a look at how to build a budget.

Build Your Budget Quickly

Most people have never tried to budget their finances. People resist budgets because they think they are too constraining. Instead of looking at a budget in this way, think of it as a road map to help you stay on the path to financial health.

Getting Started

If you have no idea how you spend your money, you need to figure that out. Write down every penny you spend during one month. Yes, I know this will be a big pain to do, but you'll be amazed by how much you learn about yourself and your spending habits by doing this.

At the end of the month, rank each of your expenditures with a number from 1 to 5. Give the number 1 to expenses that must be incurred no matter what—your mortgage or rent and other debt payments—as well as any savings you definitely want to do. Even if you just had most of your debts discharged as part of the bankruptcy, you'll most likely have some debts that you affirmed, such as a car or house payment. Give these absolute payments a number 1. You also need to eat, take medications, and do other things that maintain your daily standard of living. Rank these at number 1 as well.

Give the number 2 to important, but not required, items. For example, suppose you need to buy clothes for your job on a regular basis. Assign these items a number 2, since you need them but they're not a basic necessity of life.

Assign the number 3 to items that you wanted but could have put off a month, or things that you did socially with friends. You do need a social life, but you'll probably need to reduce these expenses to get control of your spending.

Give the number 4 to things that you probably could have skipped but wanted anyway. This might have included that new pair of shoes you didn't absolutely need, even though you loved the way they looked. Or it could be a new CD of your favorite rock band. These are things you really do want but could put off buying until you have extra cash.

Assign the number 5 to things you could have skipped completely without missing. This includes buying a cup of coffee on the way to work instead of making coffee more cheaply at home. Or it could include eating out every day instead of packing a lunch. Anything that you could easily have skipped should get a number 5.

Now list all your 1's and 2's and the total you spent on each item—for example:

Rent	$800
Food	$500
Utilities	$200

Keep going until you've finished listing all your key expenses. Now look at your 3's, 4's, and 5's. Do you really need to spend money on those items, or can you cut them?

Don't just add these items to your monthly budget. Take the time to assess how much you need each of these items and how much you want to set aside for each type of spending.

Now total that budget and see how much you need to spend on necessary items. Do you have anything left over for miscellaneous spending and saving?

If you want to get control of your spending, your best bet is to set aside a miscellaneous category and give yourself some money each month for entertainment or impulse buying. But stick to that allowable amount so you don't get yourself in trouble financially.

Credit Cleaners

> You need to make some tough decisions as you build your budget, but don't make it so confining that you find you can't live with it. Everyone needs to plan for social activity and some miscellaneous spending, but don't go overboard—be sure you can pay for it with cash.

Build Emergency Funds

Living on a budget might seem difficult at first, but once you get used to it, you'll find it's not that bad. Set aside a certain amount in a savings account each month. You may start with as little as $25 or $50 per month. Each time you don't fully spend your allotted amount in the miscellaneous category, put that extra cash in savings, too.

You'll be amazed by how quickly that savings can build. Try to build your savings as an emergency fund. That way, if something unexpected happens, you'll have the cash you need instead of being forced to take a loan to deal with the emergency.

Most people should have at least three months of monthly expenses in a savings account. If you're able to build up that kind of emergency fund, then even if you get laid off from a job, you'll have the cash you need to keep going until you find another one. If you can collect unemployment and also fall back on your emergency stash, you'll probably have enough cash for about six months.

Budgeting Together

You can't do this alone. Your spouse must work with you for your budgeting efforts to succeed. Work on budgeting together, and be sure both of you are committed to sticking to a budget.

Occasionally, one of you will want to stray from the budget. The other partner should be supportive but hold firm to the budget.

Instead of buying the item before you have the cash, agree to add a savings for the item to the budget. For example, suppose you want to buy a new TV that will cost $1,500. You can agree to set aside $100 a month for the TV. But remember, that needs to come out of the spending you would otherwise do in the miscellaneous category—you'll also have to decide what you want to give up.

Removing Temptation

After a bankruptcy, you'll find you get flooded with credit card and other solicitations. People love to lend money to someone fresh out of bankruptcy because they know your debt has been cleaned out and they know you can't file for Chapter 7 bankruptcy again for at least eight years. You've become less of a credit risk than someone who continues to make late payments and avoids credit collectors' calls.

But don't get caught up in these deals. Most of them are rip-offs with sky-high interest rates, high fees, or both. Stick to the plan to work primarily with cash.

Credit Cleaners

> You may like to take out a little revenge as you work to reduce solicitations from unwanted creditors. Stuff the junk mail they send you back into a prepaid envelope and send it back to the cred-
> itor. Hopefully, they'll get the point and take your name off the list. When solicitors have to pay for your mail and get nothing in return, the message will get through. Be sure you say no to any solicitation you return—don't just leave it blank.

While you do need to take on some credit to rebuild your credit history, as I talk about in Chapter 13, don't get caught up in these tempting offers. Instead, remove the temptation by taking steps to reduce credit card solicitations.

Blocking Mail and E-mail

You can also block direct-mail solicitations by joining the Direct Marketing Association list, which provides a Mail Preference Service. When you sign up for this service, your name is placed in a Do Not Mail file. You can start the process of signing up by going to www. dmachoice.org. You'll find easy opt-out forms for both direct mail and e-mail.

Members of the Direct Marketing Association must purge their lists of people on the Do Not Mail and Do Not E-mail lists. While this won't stop all junk mail, it will certainly slow it down.

Registration with DMA Choice.org is good for five years. When your name is put on the list, it's added to a "delete" file, which is made available to member companies.

Credit Cleaners _____

Stop getting all that annoying junk mail. Add yourself to Do Not E-mail and Do Not Mail lists at www.dmachoice.org. You won't stop everything, because not every solicitor is a member of the Direct Marketing Association, but you will reduce the volume.

Even if you register, you will continue to receive mail from companies with which you do business and from charitable or commercial organizations that do not choose to use these delete lists. You also may continue to receive e-mail from many local merchants, professional and alumni associations, and political candidates. Unfortunately, scam artists also don't use best business practices, so you can't stop all unsolicited mail and e-mail, but you can slow it down and reduce temptation.

When opting out, you have two choices:

◆ You may choose to opt out of receiving e-mail from a specific marketer.

◆ You may opt out of having your e-mail address rented or shared with other marketers.

Blocking Telemarketers' Calls

The best way to stop calls is to get on the National Do Not Call Registry. You can add your home phone number and any mobile telephone numbers that you and other family members have.

When you're listed in the National Do Not Call Registry, you get protection for your home voice or personal wireless phone numbers, but you can't get protection for business numbers. The National Do Not Call Registry prohibits telemarketers from making telephone solicitations to your home phone number or numbers, including any personal wireless phone numbers.

In addition to the federal Do Not Call lists, states have their own Do Not Call lists for residents. Contact your state's consumer protection office or public utilities commission to see if it has such a list. You can usually find contact information for these offices in the Blue Pages or government section of your local telephone directory.

Credit Cleaners

You can register your home phone number(s) on the National Do Not Call Registry by phone or by Internet at no cost. Sign up online at www.donotcall.gov or via telephone at 1-888-382-1222 (voice) or 1-866-290-4236 (TTY). You must call from the phone number you want to register.

Even if you don't sign up for one of the state or federal Do Not Call lists, a company must maintain its own list of requests. The FCC requires a person or entity placing voice telephone solicitations to your home to maintain a record of your direct request to that caller not to receive future telephone solicitations. The company must maintain a record of your Do Not Call request for five years.

While I have tried this tactic, I can't say that it works very well. Still, it can't hurt to try it. Unless your home phone number (or numbers) is registered on the National Do Not Call Registry, however, you must make a separate request to each telemarketer. Clearly, it's much more effective to use the National Do Not Call Registry.

If you do get telephone solicitation calls, clearly state that you want to be added to the caller's Do Not Call list. You may want to keep a list of persons or businesses that you have asked not to call you. Tax-exempt nonprofit organizations are not required to keep Do Not Call lists.

If you have caller ID, a telemarketer is required to transmit or display its phone number and, if available, its name or the name and phone number of the company for which it is selling products. The display must include a phone number that you can call during regular business hours to ask that the company no longer call you.

This rule applies even if you have an established business relationship with the company, and even if you have not registered your home phone number(s) on the National Do Not Call Registry. You may remember that before these rules took effect, the words "private," "out of area," or "unavailable" might have appeared on the caller ID display.

Stop Unsolicited Faxes

If you have a fax machine at home, nothing is more annoying (or costly) than getting advertising faxes. Not only do they tie up a telephone line, but they waste paper and ink.

The FCC has separate rules that prohibit unsolicited fax advertisements (under most circumstances), which are more complicated than telemarketing rules. In general, to stop unwanted fax advertisements, you must make an "opt out" request to the company faxing the junk, stating the fax number (or numbers) to which it relates; then you must send the company the telephone number, fax number, website address, or e-mail address identified on the fax advertisement.

Unfortunately, this won't necessarily stop the faxes—especially if they're scammers deliberately violating the law—but it does give you the right to sue them.

Complaining About Phone Calls and Faxes

You have the law on your side if you want to complain about telemarketers. The FCC can issue warning citations and impose fines against companies that violate or are suspected of violating the Do Not Call rules, but it does not award individual damages. If you receive a telephone solicitation that you think violates any of these rules, you can file a complaint with the FCC.

Credit Cleaners

You can file your complaint using the FCC's online complaint Form 1088 at www.donotcall.gov, or you can e-mail the FCC at fccinfo@fcc.gov. You also can call the FCC at 1-888-CALL-FCC (1-888-225-5322) voice or 1-888-TELL-FCC (1-888-835-5322) (TTY), or you can send a fax to 1-866-418-0232.

If you don't want to use the telephone or Internet options for complaining to the FCC, you can use snail mail by sending a letter to:

Federal Communications Commission
Consumer & Governmental Affairs Bureau
Consumer Inquiries & Complaints Division
445 12th Street, SW
Washington, DC 20554

If you use one of the electronic methods, you'll have a form to fill out, but if you decide to write a letter, here's what you need to include:

♦ Your name, address, e-mail address, and phone number

♦ The phone number where you received the call, and whether this number is on the National Do Not Call Registry

♦ The date and time of the call

♦ Whether the call advertised or sold any property, goods, or services

♦ Any information (including a caller ID number) to help identify the individual or company whose property, goods, or services were being advertised or sold, and whether any of this information was provided during the call

♦ Whether you or anyone else in your household gave the caller permission to call

♦ Whether you have an existing business relationship with the caller (specifically, whether you or anyone else in your household made any purchases of property, goods, or services from the individual or company that called, or made any inquiry or filed an application with the individual or company before receiving the call)

♦ Whether you or anyone in your household previously asked the caller or individual or company whose property, goods, or services are being advertised or sold *not* to call, and when you made the request

If you call the FCC, they'll ask a similar list of questions. The form you fill out deals with the same issues as well.

While you won't be able to collect individual damages, the more complaints the FCC gets about a company, the quicker and more severely it can act to stop the abusive calling. Take the time to complain when you get annoying calls after you put yourself on the Do Not Call lists.

Watching for Danger of a Credit Relapse

Like anyone addicted to something, you may find that your past compulsive shopping was an addiction that you need to watch out for all the time. If so, don't hesitate to get involved with Debtors Anonymous (http://debtorsanonymous.org) or some other self-help group.

You can't just stop doing something magically—you will be working on controlling your spending habits for the rest of your life. But some telltale signs indicate that trouble is brewing. Stop and take a second look if you find …

- ◆ You can't pay off your credit cards in full each month. You may be slipping back into the same habits you had before bankruptcy. Step through the budgeting process again to see where you're spending your money.

- ◆ You run short of cash midmonth and need to borrow money from family and friends. You'll quickly spiral downhill as your debts add up. Again, recheck your budget.

- ◆ Your necessities are greater than the amount of money you make. Either you need to figure out a way to cut back on those necessities, such as to take in a roommate, or you need to find a way to make additional money. Don't keep just going down the same road of building up debt to meet your necessities.

If you see the problems occurring and haven't yet contacted Debtors Anonymous, do so. They offer many strategies for getting your financial life back on track.

One major advantage is a sponsor who works with you personally to get you through the program. Debtors Anonymous also organizes Pressure Relief Groups and Pressure Relief Meetings to help you formulate a spending plan and get back on track with your budget.

You can get help either through local meetings or on the Internet, so don't put off making contact if you're slipping back into your old bad credit habits.

Now that we've taken a closer look at how to get control of your money, let's delve into how to repair the damage done to your credit history.

The Least You Need to Know

◆ Make a decision to regain control of your spending, and work with your family to get there.

◆ Monitor your spending and develop a budget when you have a better understanding of your money needs.

◆ Remove spending temptation by reducing the solicitations you receive daily by mail, e-mail, telephone, or fax.

◆ Watch for a spending relapse and take steps to prevent it as soon as possible by looking for help from Debtors Anonymous or other groups.

Chapter 13

Repairing Your Credit History

In This Chapter

- ◆ Report cleaning
- ◆ Error correction
- ◆ Repair timing
- ◆ Getting credit again

After you've filed for bankruptcy, you can expect a major hit to your credit score. Most people see a drop in score of at least 100 to 125 points, and rebuilding that score could take years.

But that doesn't mean you should give up on getting credit again. In fact, the sooner you start working on digging yourself out of the hole, the faster you will be able to repair your credit history and get access to credit again.

In this chapter, I show you how to repair your credit, deal with any unpaid debts, explore the legal limits to your bad credit history, and restart your financial life.

Clean Up Your Credit Report

After a credit crisis, you'll probably find that your credit report contains late payments and collection actions. You may even have a car repossessed or a home foreclosed on. All of these will lower your credit score.

You may be turned down by several lenders and give up, thinking you will never be able to get a loan, buy a house, or buy a car again. Well, that's not true, but you will need to work hard at rebuilding your credit score and being able to again get decent interest rates for loans and credit cards.

First, you must deal with the bad news. You might be terrified to look at your credit report, but bite the bullet and take a look. Your report may be better than you expect, but even if it looks like a disaster area, you shouldn't just give up.

Credit Cleaners

You can get one free copy each year of your credit report from each of the credit-reporting agencies—Equifax, Experian, and TransUnion. To get your free copy, go to www.annualcreditreport. com/cra/index.jsp. You will need to go to these websites directly and request each report there to get the report for free.

The good news is that the bad credit history can't be around forever. Every type of negative report can remain on your credit report for only a limited amount of time. This is the maximum time a negative mark can stay on your credit report:

   ◆ **Late payments**—These can be on your report for up to seven years from the time the most recent late payment was reported. If you find late payments on accounts that weren't late or those that involved a dispute about a bill, you should ask for a correction if it involves the most recent late payments.

◆ **Collections**—If any of your creditors sent your account to a collection agency for collection, you'll likely find that the collection agency also reported the debt. A collection agency action can stay on your credit report for up to seven years from the time the debt was first assigned to the collection agency.

◆ **Court judgments**—If a court made a ruling against you that involves a debt, that judgment can stay on your credit report for up to seven years from the date the court filed the ruling.

◆ **Tax liens**—If you had a tax lien and paid it off, the lien can remain on your credit report for up to seven years from the date paid. If you don't pay off a tax lien, it can remain on your credit report indefinitely.

◆ **Bankruptcies**—Your Chapter 7 bankruptcy can remain on your credit report for up to 10 years from the date you filed for bankruptcy. If you successfully complete your Chapter 13 bankruptcy, it can remain on your credit report for seven years from the date you filed the bankruptcy.

After reading about how long this information stays on your credit history, you might think you need to give up seeking credit for at least seven years. That's not true. As you add positive information and the negative information ages, your credit score will gradually improve.

Debt Dangers

Don't hire a credit-repair specialist who says he can erase these negative marks for you and give you a clean credit report. There is no legal way to get these items removed from your credit report if the information is accurate and can be proved by the creditor or collection agency.

Correcting Errors

Even if your report looks bad, you need to be certain that all the information is accurate. You may need to correct these types of errors if you've recently been through a bankruptcy filing:

- ◆ **Bankruptcy**—Be certain that the type of bankruptcy is listed on the report. If it's not, send proof of the type of bankruptcy and ask that the record be corrected. This can be critical if you filed a Chapter 13 bankruptcy because that must be removed 7 years from the date you filed for bankruptcy, as long as you successfully complete the bankruptcy; a Chapter 7 bankruptcy can stay on your record for 10 years. If the bankruptcy is on your record for longer than allowed, ask for it to be removed.

- ◆ **Accounts included in bankruptcy**—Be certain that all debts charged off are shown as being part of the bankruptcy and no longer due. Some creditors will continue to list those accounts as past due and update them periodically to keep the negative mark on your credit report longer. This is not legal, and you can stop them by having "included in bankruptcy" added to your report.

- ◆ **"Re-aged" debt**—This is a favorite game collection agencies like to play to keep your credit score low and the debt looking new. Remember that as the debt gets older, it has less of an impact on your credit score. Some collection agencies want to keep the pressure on to get you to pay, so they re-age the date by making it look more recent than it actually is. Legally, the collection agency action can be reported only for seven years from the time the agency first reported the debt. If the debt was discharged as part of the bankruptcy, send a letter to each credit-reporting agency (Equifax, Experian, and TransUnion). I talk more about how to contact these agencies shortly.

- ◆ **Old delinquencies**—If you see late payments or accounts listed as delinquent that are more than seven years old or that don't include the dates of the delinquencies, write to the credit-reporting agency and ask for your record to be corrected.

- ◆ **Paid-off debts**—If you paid off debts that are listed as unpaid, send proof of the payoff and ask for the record to be corrected.

- ◆ **Multiple accounts for same debt**—Sometimes more than one collection agency and the original creditor report to the credit-reporting agencies. If you see more than one report regarding the same debt, send proof to the credit-reporting agencies and ask for them to correct your credit report.

- ◆ **Accounts or delinquencies that aren't yours**—If accounts or delinquencies show on your credit report that are not yours, ask that they be removed. This can be a difficult situation if you were recently involved in a divorce and some of the accounts on your credit report are not yours. You can ask for the removal of an account only if you are not a cosigner of that account.

The good news is that credit-scoring formulas give more weight to your most recent credit history, so if you can build a positive credit history in two to three years, you'll start to see a significant improvement in your ability to get credit and to get better interest rate offers.

Credit Cleaners

One of the best ways to recover after bankruptcy is to rebuild your credit history as quickly as possible. That means you need to open new credit accounts and pay those accounts on time. You likely will have to use secured credit cards at first, but within a year you'll qualify for traditional credit cards.

The key is to be sure the old stuff is properly dated and will get removed from your report as soon as legally allowed. When you order a report from the credit bureau, you should see a note regarding when that information will be removed. You need to be the policeman of your credit report—no one else will watch the actions of unscrupulous creditors who use illegal ways to keep a negative mark active and up-to-date.

In addition to the major errors mentioned earlier that you could see after a bankruptcy filing, be on the lookout for some other common problems:

- **Inaccurate names**—Indicate which name on the list of names for you is incorrect. Correct the spelling of the name. If the name is one that you have never used, state that and ask that it be removed.

- **Account that is not yours**—If you see an account listed that you have never opened, indicate the account and the account number. In this situation, you will not have a full account number and can give only the partial number listed on the report. State that you have never opened the account and that it should be removed. In this situation, you also should contact the creditor involved and be sure someone has not opened an account using your identity. If you find that your identity has been used to open an account, you will need to report identity theft.

- **Payment history not accurate**—If your report shows a late payment for which you were not late, indicate that you did not pay late and ask that the information be corrected. You should include the creditor's name, account number, and late payment or payments being questioned. If you have a canceled check or other proof of paying on time, send that along with your dispute. Ask the credit-reporting agency to correct any inaccuracies.

You must carefully check the reporting dates on all these items. Dates can impact your credit score, because credit-reporting companies must remove most items within seven years. When you order a report from the credit bureau, you should see a note regarding when that information will be removed. You need to be the guardian of your credit report. Don't expect anyone else to watch the actions of unscrupulous creditors who use illegal ways to keep a negative mark active and up-to-date.

Plan Your Fix

After scrutinizing your report, make a list using two columns. One column should detail all the errors you discover, including accounts that are not legitimately yours. Any accounts that include the errors mentioned earlier can be included in this column. The second column should include accounts that are legitimately yours and unpaid.

As you start to write to the credit-reporting agencies to correct errors, start with accounts in Column 1 that show errors and have been paid off. This should include accounts you've paid off, accounts included in a bankruptcy, and accounts that aren't yours. When you get your free copy of your report, you'll see an address where you can send your letters asking for corrections.

Dispute only three to four accounts at a time. Credit-reporting agencies don't make any money working on corrections, so they don't like to handle them. You'll get better and quicker attention by not over-reporting. When the first group of account corrections is done, you can start working on another set of three or four accounts.

Debt Dangers

Don't over-report. You can upset the credit-reporting agencies, and they will find ways to slow your corrections. Since credit agencies aren't paid for corrections, their staffs do not get incentives for correcting reports. Report a maximum of three corrections per contact; that way, one employee of the credit-reporting agency won't get angry at the workload and come up with a way to punish you.

Public Records

If you do find something inaccurate in public records, you should include that in any letter you send to the credit-reporting agency asking for corrections. In addition, you should contact the county where the records are inaccurate and ask for a correction to be filed to correct the public record.

For example, if a lien was placed against your property and you paid off the underlying debt related to that lien, take the information proving that you paid the debt to the county office where the lien was placed. Show the county staff member the information and ask for help in cleaning up the record.

County clerks assist people with resolving problems with their public records every day. You will find most of them willing to help you. If not, contact an elected county official and let them know the problems you're having getting help from the staff. After you've cleaned up the public record, you can send a letter to the credit-reporting agencies asking them to correct your credit report.

Merger Mistakes

You may find that your credit report includes the credit history of someone other than you. This can happen if you have a common name or if two or more people in your family share the same name. You will need to send a letter explaining the inaccuracies and ask that the affected accounts be removed from your report.

In addition, you should send a "do-not-confuse" statement and ask that you not be confused with the same party again. In your "do-not-confuse" statement, you should include any information you have about the other party included on your report, such as name, address, phone number, place of employment, or any other identifying information you know.

"Do-not-confuse" statements are most effective if both parties involved send statements. If you know the other party, ask him to also send a statement not to confuse your records. If you don't know the other party, but do have a way to contact him, try asking him to send a "do-not-confuse" statement and give him the key information needed about you to put in the letter.

Take the time to check out your credit report at least twice a year and clean up any inaccuracies. You'll be glad you did when you next apply for a mortgage, car loan, or other credit account. You'll have a higher credit score and be able to get more attractive interest rates with a clean, accurate report than you will with one that has a lot of negative errors.

Response from Credit Bureaus

Once you send your letters, the credit-reporting agency has 30 days to respond to your letter and indicate how it will handle your challenges to the report. In that 30-day period, the agency will investigate your claims and contact the creditor that reported the information. If you have supporting data to prove your claims, it's best to send that along with your letter. In most cases, the agency will believe the creditor unless you have solid proof that the creditor is wrong.

When you get the response from the reporting agency, you may still disagree with what the creditor is reporting. In that case, you must contact the creditor directly to try to correct any inaccuracies.

You have 60 days to attempt to correct the information from the time you receive a response from the credit-reporting agency. During that period, if you're not satisfied with the response of the creditor, you can contact the credit-reporting agency again. In the response letter that you get from the credit-reporting agency, you will get detailed information about how to ask for an additional investigation.

 Credit Cleaners

If you still disagree with the information that the credit-reporting agency has verified, you have the right to submit a brief written statement indicating the nature of your dispute. The statement you submit will become part of your credit report and will be disclosed each time someone asks for the report.

Anytime a request for investigation of your credit file results in a change to that file, you have the right to ask that the corrected report be sent to any company that requested the information in the past six months. If you live in the states of California, Colorado, Maryland,

New Jersey, or New York, you can ask that the credit report be sent to any company that requested the information in the past 12 months.

Sometimes a potential or current employer gets a copy of your credit report. If the entity that requested a report was a current or potential employer, you can ask that a newly updated and corrected report be sent to any company that requested a report in the past two years.

Dealing With Unpaid Debts

You should work on repairing the accounts that you still need to pay last, but do keep a record of when these accounts were first reported to the credit bureaus. For example, you may have decided to keep your house and reaffirm your mortgage debt.

Rules are different for correcting errors for debts that are still valid, unpaid debts. If the debt involves the original creditor, you should correct any dates that are not accurate, such as inaccurate late payments.

Knowing Statutes of Limitations

In addition to credit reports, you need to understand another set of legal limits—the statutes of limitations for filing a lawsuit to collect a debt. This is important when creditors seek a court judgment to collect a debt. If they succeed in getting that judgment, they can try to collect it by going after your assets or garnishing your wages.

These statutes of limitations vary by state, but most are three to six years. Some states allow as much as 15 years for filing a suit for some types of debt.

Credit Cleaners

You can discover the statute of limitations for debts in your state at Consumer Fraud Reporting (www.consumerfraudreporting.org/debtcollectionsol.php). This is an excellent website for finding out many different types of consumer rights.

If a debt has already been paid or discharged, you don't have to worry about these laws if you want to challenge information on your credit report. But if a debt is unpaid and it survived your bankruptcy (probably because you forgot to list it), you could give notice to your creditor that you're planning to fight the debt. That may reawaken their debt-collecting activities and they could decide to file a lawsuit to collect the debt. If you don't plan to repay the debt and the debt was not discharged with the bankruptcy, you might be better off not questioning the item on your credit report and just letting it age until it finally drops off.

If you find that the statute of limitations in your state for filing a lawsuit has already passed, you can more aggressively question an old debt on your credit file. But do seek a legal opinion to be sure that any action you take doesn't restart the clock on this debt and restart the statute of limitations.

Generally, for older debt you don't intend to pay, it's best to just let this sleeping dog lie. Yes, it will remain for a number of years as a negative mark on your credit report, but renewed collection activities or a lawsuit could be much more costly in many different ways.

You may be wondering whether you should pay off the old debt. That depends on your moral values. A collector can continue to try to collect the debt even after it no longer is reported on your credit report and after the statute of limitations has run out. They won't be able to take you to court, but they can still contact you to collect.

Paying on an old debt can actually hurt your credit score, because the payment will be reported and the date for that item to be removed from your credit report is based on the most recent late payment. Also, in many states, once you make a payment, you restart the clock on the statue of limitations, which means the creditor can then take you to court.

But if you do have an unpaid debt and you want to get a mortgage on a home, you may have to pay off that debt. Often mortgage companies won't make a loan to people with old debts in their credit history. If you do want to get a mortgage before that debt is scheduled to drop off your credit report, you probably should pay it off. The sooner you do so, the better—the negative mark then can age and your credit score has time to improve. Sometimes you can negotiate with creditors and tell them you'll pay off the debt in full if they remove the item from your credit report or show the item paid in full without a negative payment history.

Adding Positive Information

The best thing you can do to improve your credit score after a bankruptcy is to build on the positive. At first, likely the only type of credit card you'll be able to get will be a secured credit card. To get that type of card, you'll have to maintain a savings or checking account with a balance that matches the amount of your credit limit.

Use this card and show that you can be responsible in paying your bills. Be sure to pay your bills on time. Gradually, as more positive information is added to your credit report, your score will improve.

Also use your credit cards sparingly. Keep your balances low so the amount of debt shown is only 10 to 20 percent of your credit limit. Even if you pay off your cards every month, the amount you charged will be reported to credit-reporting agencies. You can minimize your balance reported by paying the balance due before the end of the period. That way, the amount reported to the credit-reporting agencies will be $0.

Expect Repair to Take Years

In about a year or two after bankruptcy, you should be able to start getting credit from retail stores, such as Target and Home Depot. Also, if you've got a perfect payment record on the secured credit card, you should be able to apply for an unsecured credit card.

Continue to use credit wisely, carrying no more than about 10 to 20 percent of your allowable balance on the credit card from month to month. Using credit sparingly and showing on-time payments, you should see your score get back to what it was before the bankruptcy in about two to three years.

The Least You Need to Know

◆ Negative marks from bankruptcy don't stay on your credit report forever. The longest a negative mark can stay on your report is 10 years, and all negatives except Chapter 7 bankruptcy must drop off in 7 years.

◆ Correct errors in paid-off accounts first. Tread carefully if you want to challenge unpaid debts on your credit report.

◆ You can improve your credit score with positive reports. Start using credit again, but use it minimally and pay it off on time.

◆ Rebuild your credit by adding positive credit history after a bankruptcy. You need to show you're reformed and will pay your credit accounts on time.

Chapter 14

Getting a Job

In This Chapter

- ◆ Losing a job
- ◆ Getting hired
- ◆ Interviewing

You may be worried about losing your job or being unable to find another job after you file for bankruptcy, but don't fear: the bankruptcy code makes it illegal to discriminate against anyone who files for bankruptcy. Of course, that doesn't mean the bankruptcy on your record won't hurt your job chances.

In this chapter, I look at how bankruptcy can affect your current job and your future job searches. Then I talk about how you should handle a bankruptcy during an interview.

Possible Job Loss

Even if you don't tell your boss or future boss about your bankruptcy, he may find out if he requests your credit report. Most employers check credit history, so don't try to lie about a bankruptcy.

You're more likely to get fired because you lied than because you filed for bankruptcy. In fact, some employers think that filing for bankruptcy is less of a problem than having a lot of debt that needs to be paid. The person struggling with debt is seen as more of a risk because they may be more tempted to steal or embezzle.

So don't be afraid to tell an employer that you're filing for bankruptcy because you fear that you may lose your job. By law, an employer can't discriminate against you because you filed for bankruptcy by reducing your salary, demoting you, or taking away responsibilities.

Even though you can't lose your job, you are not obligated to inform your boss that you filed for bankruptcy. If not asked point blank about a bankruptcy filing, you should be discreet about disclosing that you've filed. It is true the Bankruptcy Code forbids an employer from discriminating against you because of a bankruptcy filing. But of course, if your boss has it in for you he or she has it in for you, and as a practical matter the anti-discrimination provisions of the Bankruptcy Code may not protect you from a particularly malicious yet resourceful employer.

If you are fired shortly after filing for bankruptcy, you might have a case against your employer under the Bankruptcy Code for illegal discrimination because of your bankruptcy. This can be true even if your employer says you were fired for other reasons, such as tardiness, dishonesty, or incompetence.

Credit Cleaners

If you think you've been discriminated against at work, contact the U.S. Equal Opportunity Commission at www.eeoc.gov or 1-800-669-4000. You also might consult with the attorney who had initially filed the bankruptcy case for you.

In most cases, if you already have the job, your employer will never learn of your Chapter 7 bankruptcy, as long as he doesn't do a periodic credit check. But if a creditor has sued you and has obtained a judgment, the creditor may *garnish wages* from your paycheck. When that happens, your employer is notified. Often that's the first clue he gets that you are in financial trouble. An employer that knows you are in trouble will be glad that you're dealing with the problem by filing bankruptcy. Employers know that work suffers when you're worried about financial problems.

def•i•ni•tion

With **garnished wages**, money is taken from your paycheck to pay a debt. Usually a court must order that the employer take those wages out of your paycheck.

If you file for Chapter 13, your employer will learn about the bankruptcy because the bankruptcy judge will likely order that your monthly payments to finish your payment plan be deducted directly from your paycheck. This is called an income deduction order.

Knowing that this will happen, talk with your boss before the order comes from the court. It's much better for him to hear it from you than to just get an order in the mail. You can explain your situation and let your boss know you're working it out.

In some bankruptcy courts, the Chapter 13 trustee will relent on this issue. If the court does relent, the income deduction requirement may be excused. You will have to agree to some extended period, during which your case may be dismissed for late plan payment without the trustee filing a motion to dismiss. If you have any doubt about your boss, and particularly if you work for a small business, you should definitely try holding out for direct plan payment without income deduction.

Security Clearances

Many jobs require security clearance, and it can be hard to get these jobs with a bad credit history. If you're a member of the armed forces or an employee of the CIA, FBI, or other governmental agency, or if your employer contracts with a federal agency, you may need to update your security clearance periodically.

You have a better chance of keeping your job if you've filed for bankruptcy than if you have bad credit and you're doing nothing to fix the problem. Credit counselors for the military and the CIA believe that a person with financial problems, particularly someone with a lot of debt, can be at a higher risk for being blackmailed than someone who has cleaned up his debt problem with bankruptcy.

When you file for bankruptcy, you get rid of the debt. This makes you a substantially lower risk. Bankruptcy can work in your favor instead of causing you a problem.

Check Bouncing

You can damage your chances to get or keep a job much more quickly by bouncing checks as you try to work around financial problems. For most companies, having a criminal record is much more damaging than filing a bankruptcy, and you can get a criminal record if you bounce checks. Credit has not been a good predictor of workplace theft; a better predictor of a possible problem is bounced checks.

Cleaning Up Your Credit Report

Your employer might ask you to clean up a credit report that looks bad. For example, if you work with a company that works with the IRS or a financial firm, you might be asked to clean up your credit problems. Also, if you deal with a lot of cash or valuables, your credit history likely will be of interest to your employer.

Bankruptcy can sometimes help you clean up problems permanently and correct any problems your employer found. Before deciding to correct a credit problem that your employer flagged using bankruptcy, be sure to discuss your possible solution with your employer. Since he's already raised the red flag, let him know you're planning to solve the problem.

You should know the following basic rules when it comes to an employer checking your credit report.

- An employer must get your permission to run a credit check. Today many employers ask you to sign a statement giving them permission to do a background check when you are hired. This includes doing a check of your credit history. You can refuse to give an employer access to your credit report, but you probably won't get offered the job if you do.

- An employer can use other credit problems to refuse to give you a job or fire you, but he can't use bankruptcy as the reason. Bankruptcy law specifically prohibits that. Since most people have trouble paying bills before filing for bankruptcy, this is often a moot point. But if an employer specifically mentions the bankruptcy when he fires you or refuses to give you a promotion, you could file a discrimination lawsuit, as mentioned earlier.

- If an employer uses something about your credit history in making a decision about hiring you, firing you, or deciding whether to give you a raise or promote you, he must give you a copy of the credit report and tell you that you have a right to dispute any incorrect information with the credit bureau.

Since employers don't usually want to bother with the legal issues related to what is found on a credit report, often they will state a different reason for making the decision and you will never know that your credit report was a factor.

If erroneous information was in your credit file, it could take you months to straighten it out, by which time someone else will be given the promotion or job you wanted. Always check your credit report at least every 12 months and correct any problems. In Chapter 13, I talk about how to repair a credit report.

Credit Cleaners

In my book *The Complete Idiot's Guide to Improving Your Credit Score*, I talk about how to maintain a good credit history. That's important not only for your financial needs, but also for job needs and insurance needs.

Problems Getting Hired

As a job applicant, you are much more likely to lose a job because you lied on your application than because you filed for bankruptcy. No federal, state, or local government agency can take your bankruptcy into consideration when making a hiring decision.

This same rule does not exist for private employers, so some people find that a past bankruptcy can come back to haunt them. Although using bankruptcy as the reason not to hire a person is discrimination, companies can easily get around this by not mentioning the fact. Some even question whether there truly is any protection given to people who lose a job because of bankruptcy. The section of the legal code involved, Section 525(b), may not stop the private employer from refusing to hire on the basis of bankruptcy filing.

You may find it difficult to get a position that requires you to handle money, including bookkeeping, payroll, accounting, or any job in the financial field.

Private employers do background checks regularly as part of the hiring process, so don't think you can hide your bankruptcy. If you're asked questions about your financial situation, answer them truthfully. You don't need to start the conversation about your bankruptcy, but don't lie about it, either.

How to Deal with Bankruptcy While Interviewing

If you're asked to give authorization for a background check, be up front about what your credit report contains. It's much better for you to tell them than for them to find out after the interview when they do the background check.

During the interview, you can talk about how the bankruptcy was a positive step in getting your financial life back together. Briefly explain how you got there. For example, if you got in trouble taking care of a sick wife or child, you may garner sympathy for your plight.

Before going to an interview, decide how you want to talk about your bankruptcy. Write down your story and practice it with family and friends. By practicing it, you'll be able tell your story honestly and confidently.

Make it clear to your future employer that you've resolved the problems that created the need for you to file bankruptcy. Let your prospective employer know that you're ready and willing to work, and that you can focus on the job and work hard.

Remember, a prospective employer is primarily concerned about whether you will do the job effectively, honestly, and efficiently. If you have a bankruptcy in your history, you may find it more difficult to prove that, but if you lie about a bankruptcy, you'll never be given the chance to prove it. You likely will get a rejection letter and never know why.

Let's take a look at common interview questions and how you can use them to reinforce that you can do the job effectively, honestly, and efficiently.

Expect to be asked some basic questions common in most interview situations. Take the time to prepare your answers at home and be ready to give your best answer that emphasizes the key points you want to make.

The three most common interview questions are:

♦ Tell me about yourself.

♦ Why do you want to work here?

♦ What are your goals?

Think of these questions as ice breakers. How you answer them sets the tone for the entire interview, so think about your responses in the quiet of your home. You can influence the flow of the rest of the interview and have a better chance that the interviewer will focus on the key things you want to present.

Use these questions to focus on your successes outside of the bankruptcy, but don't talk about yourself like you're avoiding some issue. When you practice with family and friends, tell them to watch for signs that you may be hiding something and then work on avoiding those signs in your future interviews.

The interviewer does not expect a long-winded response. Keep your initial response brief and bring out the key points you want to make. If the interviewer is interested, he will then ask a follow-up question about a specific point.

You can control the interview by saying just enough to pique the interviewer's interest and encourage his desire to learn more. That way he asks more questions about what you want to talk about.

Tell Me About Yourself.

You're not being asked to give your life history, so don't go into a long-winded story about your childhood and how you got to where you are. No one ever wants to hear your entire life story in an interview situation where they are meeting you for the first time.

Instead, think about how you can answer this question briefly and get the interviewer engaged in you as a person, not just an interviewee. If you've done your research, you should be able to pick a few experiences from your life that are relevant to the job you are seeking, point out a few job-related things, and talk about any educational background you have that is relevant.

Why Do You Want to Work Here?

With this question, the interviewer is testing your knowledge of the company and its products or services. If you do your homework, you should be well prepared to answer this question based on the research you did on the company's website.

Pick out a few things you want to talk about related to the company's goals and missions that you can tie directly to the type of position you are seeking. Don't be afraid to use the company's wording as you develop your answer to this question.

What Are Your Goals?

With this question, the interviewer is testing how long you'll stay around on the job. He probably wants to know if you just want the job for a year or two or if you think it's something you'll do for a lot longer.

Don't talk about goals you have outside the company unless they somehow relate to how you'll be staying around the area. For example, suppose you just bought a new home near the company. If you are thinking of starting a small business or doing something else once you get settled in your new home and you know that this job is just a short-term bridge to recover from the bankruptcy until you can start your business, definitely don't talk about it. Think instead about how you can answer this question to give the interviewer the impression that you will be at the job for a while. People hate going through the hiring process, so they will be less likely to hire you if they know from the start you are going to be a short-term employee.

Changing Industries After Job Loss

If your job loss after bankruptcy results in a need to change industries, you will find job hunting more difficult, especially if you are over 40. Many people who are laid off after the age of 40 find that they have a very hard time getting past the tough questions that probably aren't asked of younger candidates.

While age discrimination is against the law, there are lots of ways you can pick up clues that you may actually be sitting in front of someone that just doesn't want to hire you because you are an older worker.

The types of questions asked by an interviewer can certainly give you a clue to his or her age bias. In fact, if you are asked many of the questions you'll see next, it could be a sign that your age may be a barrier to your getting the job, not just the bankruptcy.

Tough questions for industry changers or older workers usually fall in one of two areas—questions related to your qualifications and questions related to your longevity with the company. If you are changing industries or over 40, be prepared to answer these questions before you go in. Practice your answers so you can answer the questions calmly and in a way that will be beneficial to your getting the job.

Qualification Questions

While all applicants are asked questions about their qualifications, the type of questions older workers are asked often differ. If you handle them properly, you may even be able turn a negative into a positive.

You're Overqualified. Won't You Get Bored?

You'll learn to hate this question if you start to hear it, but you must be ready with a quick answer. Deal with it effectively by talking about how impressed you are with the company and its products or services. Point out your relevant experiences that are exactly what the company needs and how your experience will let you hit the ground running. Explain that because of your experiences, you won't need much training, which will save the company time and money.

We're on the Fast Track in This Company. Can You Keep Up?

Can you imagine an employer asking someone in their 20s this question? You know it wouldn't happen, but you will hear it if you are over 40. Sure it's one of the clearest signs that age discrimination is lurking in the room, but don't get angry. Realize age discrimination is there and offset it by talking about your technical knowledge that matches what the company needs and the strategies you use to stay current on all the issues related to your field, as well as how you keep up with technology changes. You can also discuss how you dealt with rapid change in your former company, as well as how much you got done in a day on your last job. You may also want to add a story about how you stay physically fit. You can show your interviewer that you can be on the fast track by talking about your energy and attitudes.

Since You've Never Worked in This Industry, Can You Transfer Your Skills?

If you're recently laid off and your industry is in a downturn, you'll have to look outside that industry to find a job. Research the industries that interest you and prepare a list of skills that match things you've done in the past and can be easily be transferred to the skills the company you are interviewing with needs.

As you prepare for the interview, jot down some ideas that you can discuss about what you did during your career that matches what you think this company may need based on its products and services. Talk about how you think these experiences and skills will make it easy for you to quickly become a valuable employee even though you are changing industries.

Can You Relate Your Past Experiences to Our Current Business Needs?

When you change industries, you're likely to be hit with this type of question. As you prepare for the interview, make a list of past experiences that you think are relevant to the industry in you which you plan to seek employment or the type of position you are seeking.

Compare this list of past experiences with the industry or job you want to move into. Identify any skills that you think are relevant and be prepared to discuss how they would meet the needs of the hiring manager.

Don't hesitate to talk about your ability and eagerness to learn new things. Discuss how quickly you learn things and how much effort you put into anything you do. If you've taken some coursework to prepare for the job change, be sure to discuss the coursework and how that will help meet the new company's needs.

Longevity Questions

Remember, most hiring managers hate the process of hiring people and hope to find candidates who will stay around a while so they don't have to go about hiring someone again too soon. People over 40 or ones changing industries frequently will be asked about how long they plan to stay.

Expect to be asked and decide how you want to respond to longevity questions before you start interviewing. That way, when the discussion starts, your response will sound sincere and well thought out.

I See You've Been Out of Work for a While. Why?

If you've been fired after a bankruptcy and find yourself out of work for about six months or more, don't be afraid to say that. You probably don't want to talk about the bankruptcy up front, but do be prepared if it comes up.

Talk about how you spent your time and point out some activities that make you better qualified for the job, such as some training that you completed. You can also talk about how you wanted to take time off to think about what to do next, and after carefully researching your options, you've chosen to do the type of work you're applying for at the new company.

Talk about your research and make the hiring manager comfortable that you have thought things through and know what you want to do.

Don't ever give the interviewer the indication that you were looking around and this job sounded like something you wanted to try out. Be more positive than that and make your reasons for choosing the particular line of work clear and decisive.

If you took time to learn a new skill, that's a great reason to be out of work for a while. Retraining will show the hiring manager how interested you are in the job change. Talk about the skills you've learned and how you believe they will contribute to the company.

You've Moved Around a Lot. Can You Explain?

Your resumé may look very spotty because of all the job changes you had to take after losing the career position you had. Be ready to talk about and explain your reasons for your job changes.

If you've changed fields or industries, you may want to discuss how you had to work your way back up the ladder, which required job changes to broaden your knowledge or skills. If you changed jobs for promotions, be sure to point that out and how quickly you learned and moved up in your new career.

You can easily change the negative of moving around into a positive about managing and responding to change effectively, but you have to prepare and practice your response before the interview so it sounds sincere and convincing.

You've Been at One Company So Long, Can You Adapt to Our Company?

You may be someone who worked all your adult life at one company, or at least for the past 10 or 20 years before losing your job. While that makes you look like a very stable person, it also may make you look like you'll have a hard time getting used to a change.

You can handle this type of question in several different ways. One way is just to say that you're looking forward to a change and are eager to do something different. After much research, you've decided this is exactly the right type of position for you. Talk about the research you did and how you came to the decision to seek work in the field for which you are interviewing.

You can also talk about all the changes your former company went through over the years and how you thrived during those change periods. If you led the change during one or more of those periods for your former department or company, be sure to be ready to discuss your change management skills and what you learned about change. This will help convince the hiring manager that you handle change well and are worth considering for the position you are seeking.

Practice Makes Perfect

I'm sure you've heard those words from your mother as you were growing up. They couldn't be more true, especially when preparing for job interviews. Practice your answers with friends and family before you start interviewing.

In addition to the tough questions I talked about previously, also think of other questions you've been asked on previous interviews. If you were an interviewer in the past, think about the type of questions you asked and why you asked them.

Prepare a response for any question you think you might be asked. You probably will come up with a better answer if you do some research, develop your answers, and practice your responses until you are comfortable talking about the issue.

You may want to develop your own list of the tough questions and then ask family members or friends to use them to do a mock interview. If you'd like and you have the video equipment, tape your interview. Then you can watch yourself and improve your responses.

As soon as you get home after an interview, take the time to write thank-you notes to everyone that you met with during the interview process. Try to focus on one or two points that you think makes you the best candidate for the job and mention them in the thank-you note. Be sure you show your excitement about the potential job.

If you've been waiting more than a week for an answer, call back or send an e-mail to ask how things are going. Don't get offensive. Just ask what the timing for a decision will be.

You may get the bad news that someone else was offered the position. If that happens, ask if there are other positions open for which you may qualify. Also ask that you be considered for other positions in the future. Check back on a monthly basis with a quick e-mail to keep your name on top of the list and let the recruiter know you're excited about working for that company.

Now that we've explored jobs and bankruptcy, let's take a closer look at how bankruptcy will impact your ability to get loans for a house and car.

The Least You Need to Know

◆ Employers cannot discriminate against you if you file for bankruptcy.

◆ You can't lose a job if you file for bankruptcy, but employers may try to use other reasons to fire you.

◆ Employers can check your credit only if you give them permission, but if you refuse to give permission, they can refuse to hire you.

◆ Employers can fire you or refuse to hire you because of other financial difficulties, such as a bad credit history.

Chapter 15

Getting Credit After Bankruptcy

In This Chapter

- Repair credit before you buy
- Know your credit score
- Facing lenders
- Getting a student loan
- Ask a cosigner for help
- Starting a small business

When your bankruptcy case is complete and your debts have been discharged, you may wonder how long it will take before you can get a loan for a house or a car. That depends on the interest you're willing to pay. Some lenders prey on people after bankruptcy, offering loans at very high interest rates.

In this chapter, I discuss how you should work on credit repair before taking on any new loans. I talk about how much more you'll pay in interest until your credit repair is successful. I discuss lenders and how they deal with bankruptcy. Then I talk about being sure you can afford what you plan to buy. Finally, I discuss how a cosigner can help you get a loan sooner.

Repair Your Credit Before Even Trying to Buy

You will find lenders who will make loans to you immediately after a bankruptcy, but you can expect to pay rates 5 to 10 percent higher than most people. In fact, after a bankruptcy, you are considered a safer risk because you can't file for Chapter 7 bankruptcy again for at least eight years if your debts were discharged under a Chapter 7 bankruptcy. You can file a Chapter 13 bankruptcy even if there are still debts upon which you want to seek bankruptcy court protection, but you will delay the final discharge of your debts.

Your best bet is to hold off as long as possible before seeking credit, to repair your credit report and credit score. I talk about how to repair your credit in Chapter 13. Wait until your credit score is 620 before you even think about buying a house. If you need a car, you may have to pay exorbitant interest rates to get that car before you repair your credit score.

Credit Score and Interest Rates

Why wait until you repair your credit and increase your credit score? The primary reason is the amount you'll pay in interest on any loan you take. Your credit score (most commonly used is the FICO score) determines what interest rate you will pay.

During your lifetime, you could end up spending hundreds of thousands of extra dollars in interest if your credit score remains as low as it will be after a bankruptcy. You can expect your score to be in the 500s when your bankruptcy case is first completed. What does that mean?

In the following table, I show you the impact a FICO score has on the interest rate you'll be charged and the cash payments you'll need to make based on those interest rates. For example, I look at a $175,000 mortgage, a $50,000 equity loan, and a $25,000 car loan.

FICO Score Impact on Your Interest Rate and Payments

FICO Score	Interest Rate on $175,000 30-Year Mortgage	Payment on Mortgage	Interest Rate on $50,000 15-Year Equity Loan	Payment on Equity Line	Interest Rate on $25,000 60-Month Car Loan	Payment on Car Loan
720-850	4.8%	$922	4.9%	$480	6.2%	$485
700-719	5.0%	$936	5.3%	$489	7.7%	$503
675-699	5.5%	$994	6.6%	$504	9.0%	$520
620-674	6.7%	$1,124	8.0%	$527	11.7%	$552
560-619	8.6%	$1,358	7.9%	$574	15.5%	$601
500-559	9.3%	$1,446	9.4%	$614	16.0%	$609

You can see on this chart that a person with a top FICO score between 720 and 850 would be charged a 4.8 percent interest rate on a 30-year mortgage, with a monthly principal and interest payment of $922. A person with the lower score in the range of 500 to 559 would be charged 4.5 percent more in interest (9.3 percent), and the monthly payment would be $524 higher.

Yikes! Yes, you can see a tremendous difference in the amount you pay based on your credit score. The numbers I show you in the preceding figure are based on the national average interest rates available in April 2009.

Credit Cleaners

Fair Isaac has an excellent calculator you can use to view today's interest rates based on credit scores and how your payments will be impacted. After you input your loan amounts, the calculator automatically calculates the differences based on credit score. You can try this calculator at www.myfico.com/myfico/CreditCentral/LoanRates.asp.

To give you an idea of how your credit score can impact what you are able to spend over your lifetime, I developed the chart in the following figure. You can see that a person with a top credit score of 720 to 850 will spend on average $270,000 less on interest than a person with a low score of 500 to 559. That leaves people with a higher credit score a lot more money to spend on things they want.

In 2009, people with credit scores below 620 likely would have a very difficult time finding a mortgage loan even with higher interest rates—many lenders didn't lend to folks with credit scores under 620. So take your time and be sure your credit score is above 620 before you think about buying a house.

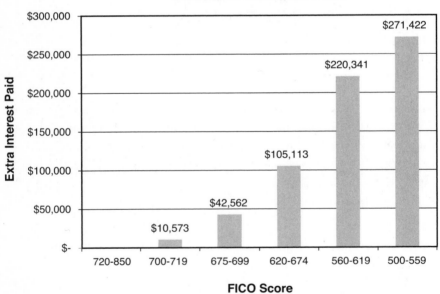

This chart shows how much extra interest a person with a low credit score would have to pay over a 30-year period.

In developing this chart based on a 30-year financial lifetime, I included a 30-year mortgage of $175,000, two 15-year equity loans of $50,000, and four car loans of $25,000. So in actuality, the interest paid over your full lifetime would be even greater. When you throw credit cards into the mix, interest costs can soar. Credit card interest rates can be as low as 7 percent for those with the best credit scores to as high as 29.99 percent or higher for people with a poor payment history.

Take the time to find out your credit score and work to improve it so you can get the best interest rates. Each credit-reporting agency has its own version of the score, so a good place to compare what you've got is www.myfico.com. You can get a free copy of your credit report once a year from each of the credit-reporting agencies at www. annualcreditreport.com/cra/index.jsp, but you will have to pay for your credit score.

Soon some of the worst abuses of the credit card industry will be banned by the new Credit Card Act passed in 2009, which takes effect February 2010. New rules include:

♦ Credit card companies will find it much more difficult to change rates, which is a dramatic shift from the existing environment where issuers can raise rates "at any time, for any reason."

♦ Credit card companies cannot increase your interest rate during an account's first year. After that first year, a credit card issuer can increase the interest rate if you are 60 days late in making a payment. If they do increase the rate, the new legislation requires them to review your account every six months and lower the rate if the situation warrants it. You will regain your older, lower interest rate if you pay your bills on time.

♦ Your creditor must pay off the balance with the highest interest rate first. Currently, credit card companies can apply the payment to the balance with the lowest interest rate.

♦ Credit card companies must disclose how much interest will be paid, as well as how much time it will take to pay off the balance if only the minimum monthly payment is made on an account.

♦ Over-the-limit fees cannot be charged unless a cardholder agrees to allow issuers to complete transactions that breach the credit limit.

- You cannot be charged a fee for paying your bill online or by phone.

- Bills must be mailed to you at least 21 days before the balance is due.

- You must get 45 days' notice (rather than 15 days) before the rate on your card can be increased.

Lenders and Bankruptcy

Some lenders develop their entire business around lending to people just out of bankruptcy. In fact, right after your debts are discharged, you'll likely receive mailings from credit card companies offering you a new card.

Be careful. Read the find print. Most of these cards or other credit offers have annual fees and extremely high interest rates. Don't get caught up in a credit scam. Although it's a good idea to get a credit card as soon as possible, to start rebuilding your credit history and your credit score, you want to minimize your out-of-pocket costs for fees and interest payments.

Start by contacting local banks and credit unions. You likely will need to open a secured credit card. That means you'll need to back up your own credit by opening a savings account of the same dollar amount as your credit line. For example, if you want a $500 credit line, you'll have to deposit $500 in a savings account.

Why would you want a secured credit card? You'll need it to rebuild your credit history. Using the card wisely and paying bills on time will improve your credit score. You'll also need a credit card to check into a hotel, travel by air, rent a car, and so on.

If your local bank doesn't have a secured card you can use, go to Bankrate.com and use its credit card search tool (www.bankrate.com/credit-cards.aspx) to compare credit card rates. Click Select By Credit Type and then click Bad Credit. Anyone fresh out of a bankruptcy case falls in the "bad credit" category. Compare the credit card offers and pick one that works for you.

You'll find prepaid credit cards and secure credit cards. For example, one prepaid card includes these benefits:

- Build your credit

- Instant guaranteed approval*—no credit check, no security deposit

- $0 activation fee—when you load your card by direct deposit

- Free direct deposit—no more check-cashing fees

- Free online bill pay—no need for expensive money orders

- No overdraft fees—no minimum balance required

- Reloadable—$10,000 balance limit

You won't qualify for a traditional credit card right away after bankruptcy, but after about six months to a year of using secured or prepaid credit cards, you will find that you can get a traditional credit card without putting up the cash first. Even after a year, you will need to carefully read the fine print on credit card offers to be sure you aren't paying too much in annual fees or getting charged too high an interest rate.

Getting Student Loans After Bankruptcy

If you ended up in bankruptcy after a job loss and need to go back to school to retrain for a new career, you're probably wondering whether or not you'll be able to get student loans after a bankruptcy. The answer is not a simple yes or no. It depends on whether or not you qualify for federal student loan programs. The type of bankruptcy you filed will also be a factor.

Credit Cleaners

If you plan to go back to school after a job loss, be certain to check with your state's unemployment program. Many states do offer assistance for training programs if you're seeking retraining to get back to work.

Don't try to determine eligibility on your own. No matter what the circumstances behind your bankruptcy, talk with the school's financial aid administrator at the school you'd like to attend and explain your situation. The financial aid administrator will be able to guide you to the student loan programs that are available, as well as the lenders who will consider an application.

You may have better luck getting aid through federal loan programs than private loan programs after a bankruptcy. Let's take a closer look at both.

Federal Loans

Generally speaking, a bankruptcy should have no impact on eligibility for federal student aid. The Bankruptcy Reform Act of 1994 amended the Federal Family Education Loan Program (FFELP) regulations dealing with loans discharged in bankruptcy. As a result of those changes, if you had FFELP, even if you previously were successful in discharging a student loan with a bankruptcy, you can still get additional aid without a requirement to reaffirm those loans prior to receiving more federal student aid.

Title IV grant or loan aid (including the Perkins loan program) may not be denied to a student who has filed bankruptcy based solely on the fact that you have filed bankruptcy in the past. Financial aid administrators are precluded from citing bankruptcy as evidence of an unwillingness to repay student loans. Schools may continue to consider the student's post-bankruptcy credit history in determining willingness to repay the loan.

As long as there are no delinquencies or defaults on student loans currently in repayment or other loans in default, you should be eligible for additional federal student loans, regardless of any past bankruptcies. But keep your loans up-to-date before applying for student aid. If some of the student's federal student loans are in default and were not included in a bankruptcy, you will not be able to get further federal student aid until you resolve the problem.

If you have a loan in default, you should contact the lender (or servicer or current holder of the loan) and set up a satisfactory repayment plan in order to regain eligibility for federal student aid. (If the loan was discharged in bankruptcy after you defaulted on the loan, it is no longer considered to be in default.)

If your parents want to help you and apply for a PLUS loan (or graduate students applying for a Grad PLUS loan), they may be denied a PLUS loan if they have an *adverse credit history.*

def•i•ni•tion

An **adverse credit history** includes having had debts discharged in bankruptcy within the past five years.

Even if your parents have an adverse credit history, they may still be eligible for a PLUS loan if they secure an endorser without an adverse credit history. If the parents are turned down for a PLUS loan because of an adverse credit history, the student may be eligible for an increased unsubsidized Stafford loan.

In case you are denied a student loan, here is the official anti-discrimination rule that you can show the financial aide administrator and ask him why you've been denied:

The anti-discrimination rules in 11 USC 525(c) include:

1. A governmental unit that operates a student grant or loan program and a person engaged in a business that includes the making of loans guaranteed or insured under a student loan program may not deny a student grant, loan, loan guarantee, or loan insurance to a person that is or has been a debtor under this title or a bankrupt or debtor under the Bankruptcy Act, or another person with whom the debtor or bankrupt has been associated, because the debtor or bankrupt is or has been a debtor under this title or a bankrupt or debtor under the Bankruptcy Act, has been insolvent before the commencement of a case under this title or during the pendency of the case but before the debtor is granted or denied a discharge, or has not paid a debt that is dischargeable in the case under this title or that was discharged under the Bankruptcy Act.

2. In this section, "student loan program" means any program operated under title IV of the Higher Education Act of 1965 or a similar program operated under State or local law.

Private Loans

Private loans can be handled differently. Since there are many different types of bankruptcies, the issues to be considered are very complex.

You should contact the financial aid administrator at the school you want to attend for advice on the impact of a bankruptcy on eligibility for private loans. You will also need to talk with the lender and provide evidence that you are a good risk.

Be prepared to explain the circumstances behind the bankruptcy. The lender may be more willing to issue a loan if you are wiling to offer to secure the loan against assets. If you are having no success getting help, you may want to consult the attorney who handled your bankruptcy.

Most bankruptcies will have an impact on eligibility for private loan programs, including some school loan programs. Many private loan programs have credit criteria that preclude people with a bankruptcy within the past 7 or 10 years from borrowing without a creditworthy cosigner. There are, however, exceptions if the bankruptcy was initiated for reasons beyond your control, such as extraordinary medical costs, natural disasters, or other extenuating circumstances. If your parent went through bankruptcy, it should have absolutely no impact on your eligibility for private loans, unless your parent is required to cosign the loans.

If the bankruptcy filing included a payout plan, even if not 100 percent, you will be at an advantage in applying for private loans. Bankruptcy filers with a payout plan, especially a 100 percent payout plan, are a better risk than most people who have gone through bankruptcy.

On the other hand, if you went the Chapter 7 route, you may have more difficulty in getting a private loan. Lenders tend to look less favorably on complete liquidations. Thus, borrowers who filed for a Chapter 11 (or Chapter 13) and had a payout plan will be more likely to get a private loan than borrowers who filed a Chapter 7.

Lenders also look at whether the borrower is able to refile for bankruptcy. Chapter 11 filers cannot immediately refile again for bankruptcy. Although any lender should know this, they may need to be reminded.

Chapter 7 filers are prohibited from refiling a Chapter 7 bankruptcy for six years. However, Chapter 13 plans have no such restriction, so a debtor can file a Chapter 7 bankruptcy, have their debts discharged, and then file a Chapter 13 within a very short time if new debt is incurred. A debtor can file an unlimited number of Chapter 13 bankruptcies. On the other hand, Chapter 13 filers are prohibited from filing a Chapter 7 immediately.

Nevertheless, lenders tend to be wary of Chapter 13 bankruptcies because a high percentage of them are converted to Chapter 7 cases or are dismissed because the debtor is unable or unwilling to continue with the payments established under the Chapter 13 repayment plan.

Seek a Cosigner

Building your credit score high enough to get reasonable interest rates to buy a car, or any major purchase, will take two to three years. You may find that it takes four to five years to get someone to consider lending you money for a house, especially if your bankruptcy included a home foreclosure.

You may be able to speed the process of getting loan approval by asking a family member or friend to cosign a loan. You're asking for a huge favor because that person also puts his or her credit rating on the line. If you don't make the payments, your cosigner will be asked to do so. So don't even think about asking for a cosigner if you think there's any risk that you can't afford to make the payments.

Debt Dangers

Seeking a cosigner should be your last resort, not your first option. The last thing you want to face is telling a family member that you must default on a loan for which they are a cosigner. Families have broken up over less.

The big advantage of a cosigner is that you then get the benefit of the cosigner's higher credit score when applying for the loan. Your interest rates will be lower, and you'll have a much better chance of getting loan approval.

Starting a Small Business

Your bankruptcy may have been the result of a job loss, and you're thinking of starting a new business. You probably will not be able to seek the help of the Small Business Administration until you actually get the business off the ground and improve your credit history.

A U.S. Small Business Administration loan is actually a private loan guaranteed by the government and made to small companies and start-up entrepreneurs with viable business plans who couldn't get commercial loans. You will have to undergo a criminal background check and demonstrate creditworthiness. If you have a history of insolvency or are perceived to be a credit risk, you're unlikely to qualify for a loan of any kind.

So if you do want to start a business, you'll need to count on family and friends to help you out initially after a bankruptcy. Consider taking in a partner who is willing to put up most of the money but is not interested in the day-to-day operations of running a business. Or you can find a partner who complements your skills.

For example, suppose you are thinking of starting a business as a painting contractor. You have the painting skills but not the skills for promoting and getting clients. Your friend is a good talker and knows how to generate business. You already have most of the equipment you need for small jobs, so you can start the business without a lot of money up front.

Any type of business that you can start based on existing skills and existing equipment will be the easiest to get off the ground. As you build the business, you will need new equipment to be able to take on bigger and better jobs. Use the time while you're building your business to also demonstrate your creditworthiness.

After three to four years, if you develop a well-run business that is making money, you'll have a much better chance of getting a commercial or small business loan.

> **Debt Dangers**
>
> Even if you qualify and have an excellent credit history, you must jump through lots of hoops to get a small business loan. They are among the most difficult types of loans to get, so don't count on success.

Make your plans for growth without depending on the option of getting a small business loan. Build your business and seek help from friends, family, or possibly private investors. As you work for people, if they like your work they may be willing to invest in your business.

But be careful about taking on investors. Be sure they are people you want to work with over a long period of time. Remember, people get even more picky about how things are done if their money is on the line.

Now that we've looked at the impact a bankruptcy can have on buying a house or a car, let's look at how you can manage your credit with a spouse, especially if your spouse didn't file bankruptcy.

The Least You Need to Know

◆ Credit scores determine the interest rates you pay. Repair your credit report before applying for a major loan, and you'll improve your credit score.

◆ Bankruptcy will not make it impossible to get a student loan, but you may need to jump through some extra hoops.

◆ Seek a cosigner if you must borrow money before you have time to repair your credit score.

◆ You will find it very difficult to get a small business loan with a bankruptcy in your credit history.

Chapter 16

Managing Your Credit with a Spouse

In This Chapter

- ◆ Separate credit history
- ◆ Loan applications
- ◆ No joint accounts

When filing for bankruptcy, if most of the debts are separate debts of just one spouse, your life after bankruptcy will be much easier if just one spouse with the debt files for bankruptcy. Whether or not this strategy will succeed depends on the laws in your state.

If you got married after one spouse filed bankruptcy, it's crucial to keep your credit lives separate until the bankruptcy drops off his or her record. By doing so, you'll find it easier to buy a car or a house or do other things you want to do that involve using credit.

In this chapter, I talk briefly about the key state laws that impact your life as a couple before, during, and after filing bankruptcy. Then I talk about the importance of keeping your credit files separate and how to make sure you do that. Finally, I talk about applying for loans in one spouse's name and how critical it is to avoid taking on joint credit accounts.

Key State Laws Impacting Couples and Bankruptcy

If you're married and thinking about filing for bankruptcy, first look at who owns the debt. If most of your debt is in both names, you have no option: you'll need to file for joint bankruptcy. But if most of the debt is separate debt and only one spouse owns that debt, a separate bankruptcy may be your best choice.

Debt Dangers _____

In most states, your homestead exemptions will protect your house in a bankruptcy filing, as long as you can reaffirm the debt and continue to make the payments after the bankruptcy. Don't reaffirm your debt unless you truly know you can make the payments. You won't be allowed a do-over after your bankruptcy case is discharged. After a Chapter 7 bankruptcy, you can't file for Chapter 7 bankruptcy again for eight years.

You can find out how much protection your homestead exemptions will give you by looking at Appendix C. For example, suppose your state allows an exemption of $50,000. Your home is worth $300,000 and your outstanding debt totals $250,000. Your $50,000 of equity in the home will be protected by that homestead exemption and you won't lose your house as long as you can make the payments. Your equity will also be untouchable by your creditors. I talk more about how the homestead exemptions work in Chapter 8.

In addition to homestead exemptions, some states have strong protections for couples when only one spouse files for bankruptcy. A couple can use the strongest of those protections by holding title to marital assets in tenancy by the entirety. If you live in one of these states and hold your title in tenancy by the entirety, your home's value could be protected 100 percent if only one spouse owes the debt.

Tenancy by the Entirety

Seventeen states (and the District of Columbia) allow spouses to own property in tenancy by the entirety: Delaware, Florida, Hawaii, Illinois, Indiana, Maryland, Massachusetts, Michigan, Missouri, North Carolina, Ohio, Pennsylvania, Rhode Island, Tennessee, Vermont, Virginia, and Wyoming. In these states, even if one spouse files for bankruptcy, you don't have to worry about losing your home as long as you continue to make the payments on your home—even if you have hundreds of thousands of dollars of equity in that home.

Community vs. Common-Law Property States

Another set of laws that impact the strategy of who in a married couple should file for bankruptcy involve common-law property states and community property states. Marital debt is handled differently, depending on these laws.

Community Property Laws

Nine states have community property laws: Arizona, California, Idaho, Louisiana, Nevada, New Mexico, Texas, Washington, and Wisconsin. Couples in Alaska can elect to have their property treated as community property if they sign an agreement to that effect.

If you live in a community property state, your debts incurred separately during a marriage are considered "community debts," even if only one of you signs a debt agreement. This means that even if you don't know that your spouse signed the paperwork, you're still responsible for the debts. This rule makes it nearly impossible to file for bankruptcy separately if most of your debts were taken on during the marriage.

So if you are in a community property state and bankruptcy is being contemplated, be certain to talk with your attorney to find out if there's any advantage to filing for bankruptcy separately.

Debt Dangers

If you live in a community property state, your spouse can go out and buy a car without you and you'll still be held liable for the debt. Anytime your spouse comes home with a major purchase, be sure you know how he or she paid for it.

Common-Law Property States

The rest of the states are common-law property states. In these states, either spouse who incurs debt before getting married is considered to be taking separate debt. Debts incurred during the marriage could be either separate or joint debt.

If you take debt jointly by opening a joint account or the creditor considered credit information from both spouses in making the loan, the debt is considered joint debt. Even if only one spouse took the loan, if the debt was for necessary items such as food, clothing, and child-care expenses, the debt could be considered a joint debt.

Debt Dangers

Even if you live in a common-law property state, you could still be stuck with liability on a debt that was taken just by your spouse if that debt is for necessary items used by both of you. Always keep the lines of communication open when it comes to debt during a marriage.

Any debt that does not meet the criteria mentioned is handled as a separate debt in a bankruptcy filing. So if you think you can show that most of your debt is separate debt and only one spouse needs to file for bankruptcy, your life will be a lot easier after a bankruptcy if only one spouse files.

For example, suppose that only your spouse had credit card accounts that need to be discharged with a bankruptcy, but you plan to reaffirm your mortgage, which is your only joint debt. In this scenario, as long as your state homestead laws protect your home, you should talk with your attorney about possibly having just one of you file bankruptcy.

Credit Cleaners

Couples have a big advantage in a common-law property state over a community property state because it's easier for them to benefit from separate bankruptcy filings. If only one spouse files for the bankruptcy, the other spouse can maintain a better credit rating, which makes it easier for the couple to get credit after a bankruptcy.

Keeping Credit Files Separate

From the first day of marriage, keep your credit files as separate as possible. Although you may need to take joint debt periodically, such as for a major purchase like a house, keeping the rest of your credit life separate is a good idea for many reasons.

If one of you is better at paying bills on time, that person's credit history will be better and the couple can more easily use that credit history. Of course, you also can put the more fiscally responsible spouse in charge of paying the bills on time. That will be best for both of you because you'll both need good credit histories to buy a house.

Credit Cleaners

Keep your credit files as separate as you can during a marriage. You will have more flexibility if there is a financial problem down the road. This can be especially true if one spouse is better at paying bills than the other.

Even if your debt is always paid on time, a big advantage of separate debt, especially if both spouses hold full-time jobs, is that you can build a large amount of available debt. That is, each of you can have your own credit cards and get your own credit lines.

As you show that you can handle credit wisely, those lines will gradually increase. Your credit score is based on the percentage of debt that you use. For example, you get the best credit score with a debt-utilization ratio of between 10 and 20 percent. If you have only $1,000 in credit available, you can charge only $200 to be within that debt-utilization ratio. But if you have a credit line of $20,000, you can use between $2,000 and $4,000 of that credit and still get an excellent credit score.

One of the biggest mistakes couples make is to take all their credit together. This gives them no leeway to manage an emergency using credit cards. Also, if the couple decides to divorce at some point in the future, joint credit cards will all need to be closed. At that time, both of you will need to restart your credit life. Although I'm not saying you should plan for divorce, unfortunately, a high percentage of marriages do end up in divorce—why not protect your credit life?

 Credit Cleaners _____

You'll find it much easier to build your credit separately, as you get credit line increases for paying on time. Carefully charge items equally to maintain good credit for both of you. If for some reason you have an emergency and must use more of your available credit for a few months until you can pay it off, put those charges on just one of your credit records. That way, only one of your credit scores will be negatively impacted, and you'll still maintain at least one top credit score in the family.

In the future, the fact that you keep separate credit histories and use separate credit cards may make it easier for just one of you to face bankruptcy, so you can ruin just one credit history. Recovering after bankruptcy can be much faster if one of you still has a good credit rating.

Applying for Loans in One's Name

You may think it's difficult to apply for credit under only one spouse's name, but you'll find it very easy. But if you're applying for a mortgage and need the income of both of you, you may find this harder to do.

Before the collapse of the housing market, when it was easier to get loans, couples didn't find it hard to apply for mortgages under only one spouse's name. When I married my current spouse, he had filed for bankruptcy just before we married. His credit history was a mess, but we were still able to buy a house.

We bought the house using my excellent credit history. I'm a fanatic about paying bills on time. Since I'd worked with the same bank for about 20 years, it was easy for me to get a *no-document loan* and state household income without needing to prove it. That way, I could include my husband's income in the calculations but not have to prove it on paper.

def•i•ni•tion

A **no-document loan** or stated-income loan is a loan for which you don't have to prove the income. These loans have become known as liar loans because so many people overstated their income between 2006 and 2008.

If the bank had checked his credit history, we probably would not have gotten the loan—or it would have been at a much higher interest rate. Since I'd had at least five mortgages with the same bank over the years, my known history helped make this happen. So sometimes getting the best rate is not your only goal. Building a strong relationship with one bank can help in situations like these.

The mortgage broker did know why we were applying for the loan using only my credit history. Unfortunately, our tactic likely would not have worked in 2009 because no-document loans are difficult, if not impossible, to find these days. Still, if you have a strong relationship with a local bank or credit union, it doesn't hurt to try.

Even if you can't use a no-document loan, work with a mortgage broker or loan officer to develop the best strategy to apply for a loan if one of you has a terrible credit history. Sometimes a mortgage broker can help you work up a letter of explanation that will enable you to go forward with the loan.

For example, suppose the reason you needed to file the bankruptcy was that you incurred tremendous medical bills caused after an automobile accident. Your spouse had to file bankruptcy to get a fresh financial start, but once those bills were discharged, he had no debt left. A bank may be willing to consider a loan under those circumstances, if you can prove that the hardship that caused the bankruptcy is now history.

You may find that you have to wait a few years before you can get a mortgage if one spouse filed bankruptcy. If so, use the time to save up a larger down payment. That will make it easier for you to get a loan in the future—plus, you'll have lower mortgage payments.

The larger your down payment, the easier it will be for you to get a loan even if one spouse has terrible credit. For example, if you have 30 to 50 percent to put down, you can often get a loan even after filing bankruptcy, but you will have to pay much higher interest rates.

Even if you have to wait, it usually takes about three years to rebuild credit after a bankruptcy. My spouse's credit score is back up over 700, even though his bankruptcy is just three years old. I talk about how to repair your credit score in Chapter 13.

 Debt Dangers

Don't let a low credit score stop you from applying for debt as long as one of you has a good score. You can apply for a mortgage on a house in one spouse's name even if both of you plan to be on the deed. I've done this several times over my lifetime. Splitting the ownership and the debt this way will enable you to get the mortgage in just one name: that of the spouse with the better credit score.

Don't Take on Joint Credit Accounts

Use joint credit accounts sparingly during marriage. The only reason to take a joint credit account is if you need both incomes to qualify for the debt.

Otherwise, your best bet is to take turns opening an account for a specific purpose—for example, taking a credit card to get 0 percent for a year on a major project, such as new countertops from Home Depot. Also, be sure you pay off that purchase before the 12 months are up. Most of these 12-month, 0-percent deals continue to build up interest through the year.

If you don't pay the full amount before the end of the 12 months, you'll be socked with a huge bill for interest as well as the original purchase. Interest charges usually build up at a rate higher than 20 to 25 percent. Check your interest rate and watch your monthly billing to see how much interest is building up on the purchase amount. As long as you pay the bill in full before the end of the special deal, you'll never pay any of those interest charges.

Aside from special purchases, you each should have no more than two credit cards. Try to always pay off your credit cards in full each month, but avoid leaving debt on your card that totals more than 20 percent of your total available debt.

Take turns charging on your cards, to keep your debt levels low, and assign the person who is best about paying bills on time the job of paying those bills. In today's credit environment, one late payment can be a disaster.

If you're late with one payment, a credit score can drop by as much as 100 points. Your credit card companies can hike your interest rates to 29 percent or higher. Congress is considering bills to get some of this under control, but no one knows what the bills will finally look like.

Your best bet is to avoid having to worry about credit card penalties and what will happen to your interest rates. Always pay your bills on time and use credit wisely, and it won't matter.

The Least You Need to Know

- ◆ Keep your credit history separate throughout marriage. This will help if you need to file bankruptcy or end up filing for divorce.

- ◆ If you need to file bankruptcy, having only one spouse file can make recovery after bankruptcy much easier, as long as you keep your credit files separate.

- ◆ State laws vary. Check with your attorney about whether you can file separately.

Appendix A

Glossary

bankruptcy trustee   A person the bankruptcy court appoints to oversee a bankruptcy. In a Chapter 7 case, the trustee seeks to find as much cash as possible to repay your creditors. This can include seizing assets and selling them. In a Chapter 13 case, he or she collects three to five years of your Chapter 13 plan payments, distributing those payments to your creditors in accordance with your confirmed Chapter 13 plan.

breach of fiduciary duty   Failing to live up to a duty of trust, such as one to manage property or money for someone.

collateral   Property that is pledged as security for a loan. For example, when you buy a house and agree to make monthly mortgage payments, you pledge that home as collateral. If you don't make the payments, the bank can foreclose on the home and take possession.

confirmation   A ruling by the bankruptcy judge that approves your Chapter 13 bankruptcy plan.

cramdown   A bankruptcy judge lowers the amount due on your mortgage to the home's current market value. Congress is considering making this an option in a change to the bankruptcy laws.

discharge   A court order issued at the end of a bankruptcy case that legally relieves you of your personal liability for the debts.

embezzlement   Taking property for which you have responsibility and using it for yourself.

fraudulent income taxes   Taxes due because you didn't file a return or taxes due because you intentionally avoided your tax obligations.

garnished wages   Money that is taken from your paycheck to pay a debt. Usually a court must order that the employer take those wages out of your paycheck.

homestead exemption   The amount of equity you have in your primary residence that is protected from bankruptcy. Each state sets its own rules on how much you can claim as a homestead exemption. Some states do allow you to simply incorporate the federal exemptions.

larceny   Theft.

liquidate   To pay down all your debt. You may need to sell some of your property to pay down that debt. In Chapter 7, a trustee disposes of all of your nonexempt property to pay toward your debt.

median income   The dollar figure for a salary that is exactly in the middle of income earners within the state of filing, based on household size. The same numbers of people earn less than the median as those who earn more.

no-document loan   A loan for which you don't have to prove your income. These loans have become known as liar loans because so many people overstated their income between 2006 and 2008. They are also referred to as stated income loans.

reaffirmation agreement   Agreement with a creditor after a bankruptcy filing, and the agreement to repay the debt after the bankruptcy has ended.

Schedule C   The form attached to your individual income tax Form 1040 to report the profit and loss from a business.

secured debt   Debt for which you put up collateral, such as your house, when you take a mortgage. If you don't make the mortgage payments, the bank can repossess your house. The same is true when you take a car loan or any other loan in which you agree to give up certain real or personal property if you fail to pay the loan.

sole proprietors   Businesspeople who start a business by themselves without making use of a corporation or partnership.

stated income loan   *See* no-document loan.

tenancy by the entirety   The way couples can hold property in some of the states. When one spouse dies, the surviving spouse automatically owns 100 percent of the property. In most cases, this type of property is not part of the bankruptcy estate if only one person files.

unsecured debt   Debt that is not backed by an asset. For example, most credit card debt and medical debt has no underlying asset securing that debt. If you can't pay, no asset can be seized and sold.

wildcard exemptions   Allow you to keep a certain dollar amount of assets. You decide which assets you want to use the exemptions to save. This varies state by state.

Resources

In this resources section, you'll find sources for additional reading, contact information for key sections of the bankruptcy courts, and other key governmental and nongovernmental websites. I also include some basic information if you need help with paying for your medical needs.

Further Reading

The Complete Idiot's Guide to Improving Your Credit Score (Alpha, 2007) is an excellent book for information on how to repair your credit and maintain a good credit history. That's important not only for your financial needs, but also for job needs and insurance needs.

Bankruptcy Courts

The primary website for official information about filing for bankruptcy is www.uscourts.gov. Here are some key links to help you find things on that website:

◆ If you do want to do it yourself, look for basic information on the website for the bankruptcy court where you will be filing (www.uscourts.gov/courtlinks).

◆ You can find bankruptcy resources at the U.S. Courts website (www.uscourts.gov/bankruptcycourts/resources.html), as well as detailed information about bankruptcy basics.

◆ Take a look at the forms that you'll need to file with bankruptcy court by downloading them from the U.S. Courts website (www.uscourts.gov/bkforms/bankruptcy_forms.html).

◆ You can find the administrative expenses multiplier for your district at www.usdoj.gov/ust/eo/bapcpa/20090315/bci_data/ch13_exp_mult.htm. These multipliers are set by bankruptcy court districts.

◆ The U.S. Trustee website lists counseling agencies approved by the bankruptcy court. You can search for a counseling agency near you at www.usdoj.gov/ust/eo/bapcpa/ccde/cc_approved.htm.

◆ You can find an approved budget-counseling session by going to the U.S. Trustee website (www.usdoj.gov/ust/eo/bapcpa/ccde/de_approved.htm).

Other Key Government Websites

In addition to information that you can find at the U.S. Courts and U.S. Trustee websites, other government agencies have useful links:

◆ You can check the median income for your state at the Census Bureau website (www.census.gov/hhes/www/income/statemedfaminc.html).

◆ You can find the IRS's allowable costs for food, clothing, and other items at www.irs.gov/businesses/small/article/0,,id=104627,00.html.

- You can find the IRS's allowable transportation costs at the IRS website. The IRS divides transportation into two categories: general transportation (includes car maintenance or public transportation) and transportation ownership expenses (includes car loans or leases). To calculate allowable monthly expenses, use the numbers for general transportation at www.irs.gov/businesses/small/article/0,,id=104623,00.html.

- If you think you've been discriminated against at work, contact the U.S. Equal Opportunity Commission (www.eeoc.gov) by phone, at 1-800-669-4000.

- You can find a housing counselor by going to the website of the U.S. Department of Housing and Urban Development (HUD), at www.hud.gov/foreclosure. There you will find information about seeking help to avoid foreclosure, as well as information about local counselors who can help you.

- If you're having trouble paying your mortgage, you can get free assistance from a HUD Housing Counselor. You can search online for a counselor near you at www.hud.gov/offices/hsg/sfh/hcc/hcs.cfm, or you can call 1-800-569-4287 to find a Housing Counselor near you.

Nongovernmental Agencies

You'll also find some nongovernmental associations that will help you through a bankruptcy, assist with credit problems, or help deal with the possible loss of your home.

- A good source for help with mortgage problems is the Homeowner Crisis Resource Center of the NFCC, 1-866-845-2227.

- You can find information about free legal help through the American Bar Association's Legal Help page (www.abanet.org/legalservices/findlegalhelp/home.cfm) or the Legal Services Corporation (www.lsc.gov), in addition to your state's local bar association.

- The most respected source for locating a nonprofit credit counselor is the National Foundation for Credit Counselors (www. nfcc.org).

Websites for Further Research

You'll find these websites helpful for finding additional information about bankruptcy and related topics.

- If you think compulsive spending drove you to bankruptcy, think about joining Debtors Anonymous (www.debtorsannonymous. com) for support. They offer support groups online to help you get control of your spending.

- You can find out the statute of limitations for debts in your state at Consumer Fraud Reporting (www.consumerfraudreporting. org/debtcollectionsol.php). This is an excellent website for learning about many different types of consumer rights.

- The price at which your home could sell today is known as the market value. If you're not sure what homes are selling for in your area, you can talk to a realtor or find estimated prices on Zillow (www.zillow.com).

- Each year, you can get one free copy of your credit report from each of the credit-reporting agencies: Equifax, Experian, and TransUnion. To get your free copy, go to www. annualcreditreport.com/cra/index.jsp. You must request each report directly from this website to get them for free.

- After bankruptcy, you can compare credit card options at Bankrate.com and use its credit card search tool (www.bankrate. com/credit-cards.aspx) to compare credit card rates. Click Select By Credit Type and then click Bad Credit. Anyone fresh out of a bankruptcy case falls in the Bad Credit category. Compare the credit card offers and pick one that works for you.

- You can monitor your credit-repair efforts after bankruptcy at www.myfico.com. Take the time to learn your credit score and work to improve it so you can get the best interest rates.

◆ Fair Isaac has an excellent calculator you can use to view today's interest rates based on credit scores and determine how your payments will be impacted. After you input your loan amounts, the calculator automatically figures the differences based on credit score. You can try this calculator at www.myfico.com/myfico/CreditCentral/LoanRates.asp.

◆ If you're 62 or older and need to tap the equity in your home, you may want to consider a reverse mortgage. You can find out more about the pros and cons of reverse mortgages at AARP's website (www.aarp.org/money/personal/reverse_mortgages/).

Getting Assistance with Health Care

Some charities will also help people with certain conditions. These charities include Caring Voice Coalition, Chronic Disease Fund, The HealthWell Foundation, National Marrow Patient Assistance Program, National Organization for Rare Disorders, and Patient Advocate Foundation's Co-Pay Relief. Following is a brief summary of the types of support each provide.

Caring Voice Coalition

The coalition can help you with the cost of some of your prescriptions if you have one of the following conditions: pulmonary arterial hypertension, idiopathic pulmonary fibrosis, alpha-1 antitrypsin deficiency, chronic granulomatus, or Huntington's disease. You can find out more at www.caringvoice.org or by calling 1-888-267-1440.

Chronic Disease Fund

This fund offers two types of assistance. One program, Patient Financial Assistance, provides copay assistance for certain drugs (as long as your drug plan covers the drug) if you cannot afford the copay. It also offers a Free Drug Program to people who meet income, asset, and medical condition guidelines.

Help covers these conditions: age-related macular degeneration, alcohol dependence, ankylosing spondylitis, asthma, breast cancer, colorectal cancer, growth hormone deficiency, multiple myeloma, multiple sclerosis, myelodysplastic syndrome, non-small-cell lung cancer, and psoriasis.

You can find more information at www.cdfund.org or by calling 1-877-968-7233.

The HealthWell Foundation

This foundation will help you pay your drug copays if you have insurance, or help you pay your monthly premiums if you are eligible but can't afford to pay for insurance. You must meet income criteria to qualify for help. Income criteria is based on multiples of the poverty level.

Diseases the foundation supports include acute porphyries, age-related macular degeneration, anemia associated with chronic renal insufficiency or chronic renal failure, ankylosing spondylitis, asthma, breast cancer, carcinoid tumors, chemotherapy-induced anemia or nutropenia, colorectal carcinoma, cutaneous T-cell lymphoma, head and neck cancer, Hodgkin's disease, idiopathic thrombocytopenic purpura, immunosuppressive treatment for solid organ transplant recipients, iron overload as a result of blood transfusions, non-Hodgkin's lymphoma, non-small-cell lung cancer, psoriasis, psoriatic arthritis, rheumatoid arthritis, secondary hyperparathyroidism, and Wilms' tumor.

You can find out more at www.healthwellfoundation.org or by calling 1-800-675-8416.

National Marrow Patient Assistance Program and Financial Assistance Fund

This program provides assistance for the cost of prescription drugs that must be taken as part of recovery after a marrow transplant. To qualify, you must have used the National Marrow Patient Assistance

Program's donor registry to find your marrow transplant donor. The donor also must not be a family member.

You can find out more about this program at www.marrow.org or by calling 1-888-999-6743.

National Organization for Rare Disorders

This organization can help you obtain prescriptions that you can't afford or help pay for drugs not yet on the market. The organization's database includes more than 1,000 diseases.

To see which diseases this program includes, or to learn more about the organization, go to www.rarediseases.org or call 203-744-0100. You can leave a voicemail message at 1-800-999-6673.

Patient Advocate Foundation's Co-Pay Relief

This foundation will pay your full copay for prescriptions that your insurance covers, as long as you take them to treat a medical condition of interest to the foundation. Eligible conditions include breast, lung, prostate, kidney, colon, pancreatic, and head/neck cancers; malignant brain tumors; lymphoma; sarcoma; diabetes; multiple myeloma; myelodysplastic syndrome (and other pre-leukemia diseases); osteo-porosis; selected autoimmune disorders; and secondary issues as a result of chemotherapy treatment.

You can find more information about this foundation at www.copays. org or by calling 1-866-512-3861.

Appendix C

State-by-State Homestead Exemption Rules

Each state passes laws that allow exemptions to shield certain types of property from your creditors when you file bankruptcy. These protections may help you keep your home, car, clothing, tools, and other important property when you file for bankruptcy. You'll find the basic household and personal property exemptions for each state, but always check with your attorney for more specifics about your assets and which ones you can keep if you file for bankruptcy. States do change bankruptcy laws periodically—for the most up-to-date list of exemptions, check out BankruptcyAction.com.

Federal Exemptions

You can get a homestead exemption of up to $20,200, and you can use up to $10,125 not used toward the homestead exemption to protect any other property. In addition, personal property—including animals, crops, clothing, appliances, books, furnishings, household goods, and musical instruments—is exempt up to $525 per item, up to a total of $10,775. Jewelry is exempt up to $1,350. A motor vehicle is exempt up to $3,225. Implements, books, and tools of the trade are exempt up to $2,025. There's also a wildcard category of up to $1,075. Many states with lower exemptions do not allow residents to use the federal exemption rules.

If you have moved in the past 1,215 days (3.3 years), you may not be able to use the homestead exemption rules in the state where you currently reside. Instead, you must use the federal rules that allow you to exempt up to $125,000 in homestead exemption, regardless of state law providing for a larger or unlimited exemption if you moved recently.

This limitation comes into play more often if you move to a state with higher exemptions. For example, if you move from one state with an unlimited dollar amount, such as Florida, to another with an unlimited dollar amount, such as Texas, you would still be limited to a $125,000 homestead exemption if the move was less than 1,215 days before you filed bankruptcy. If you've lived in your state longer and have a higher homestead exemption, you can use your state's exemption rules.

But if your debtor claim arises from violations of federal or state securities law, RICO, fiduciary fraud, or certain crimes or intentional torts, the cap is $125,000, regardless of when the property was acquired.

Rollovers of exempt homestead interests are not allowed even if those interests were exempt in both states. Thus, a debtor who moves from Texas to Florida retriggers the 1,215-day period, despite the fact that both states have unlimited homestead exemptions.

Alabama

You can get a homestead exemption of up to $5,000 for property up to 160 acres in area. That means that up to $5,000 of the equity in your home can be protected (a mobile home or similar dwelling constitutes a homestead if it is your principal residence). If you have more than $5,000 in equity and you file for Chapter 7 bankruptcy, the bankruptcy court could order your home sold to pay off your debtors. Only the state exemptions are allowed. Residents cannot take advantage of the higher federal bankruptcy exemptions. Wages of up to 75 percent of your weekly, disposable earnings are exempt. There is no specific exemption for automobiles. Up to $3,000 in the value of all other personal property can be exempt. There is no limit on personal keepsakes and family pictures.

Alaska

You can get a homestead exemption to protect up to $67,500 in the equity of your home. If you have more than $67,500 in equity and you file for Chapter 7 bankruptcy, the bankruptcy court could order your home sold to pay off your debtors. Only the state exemptions are allowed. Residents cannot use federal bankruptcy exemptions. Wages of up to $438 weekly are exempt. You can exempt up to $3,750 for one motor vehicle, not exceeding $25,000 in value. Up to $3,750 in the value of household goods, clothing, books and musical instruments, and family heirlooms can be exempted. There are also exemptions for jewelry up to $1,250 and for professional books and tools of the trade up to $3,500.

Arizona

You can get a homestead exemption of up to $150,000. This means that up to $150,000 of the equity in your home (which includes a mobile home) can be protected. If you have more than $150,000 in equity and you file for Chapter 7 bankruptcy, the bankruptcy court could order your home sold to pay off your debtors. Only the state exemptions are allowed. Residents cannot use federal bankruptcy exemptions. Wages of up to 75 percent of your weekly, disposable earnings are exempt. One automobile up to $5,000 in value can be exempted (up to $10,000 if you are disabled). Up to $4,000 in the value of household furniture, furnishings, and appliances can be exempt. There's also an exemption of up to $500 for clothing. Engagement and wedding rings are exempt up to $1,000. Tools of the trade are exempt up to $2,500.

Arkansas

You can get an unlimited homestead exemption as long as your lot size is no more than ¼ acre in the city or 80 acres elsewhere where you file for Chapter 7 bankruptcy; otherwise, the bankruptcy court could order your home sold to pay off your debtors. Since you can use federal or state exemptions rules, check with your attorney to find out which rules are better for you. Up to $200 of clothing is exempt. Up to $1,200 of equity in your car is exempt. Exemptions are also available for up to $1,000 in life insurance and disability payments, and up to $20,000 in IRA contributions, as long as they were made more than a year before the bankruptcy. Up to $750 in tools you use for your trade can also be exempt.

California

You can get a homestead exemption of up to $75,000 for a family member living with one or more non-owner family members. People 65 or older, disabled people, and people over 55 with an annual gross income of under $15,000 (if single) or under $20,000 (if married) can get an exemption of up to $150,000. If you're not in one of these categories, the homestead exemption is $75,000. Only the state exemptions are allowed. Residents cannot use federal bankruptcy exemptions. Paid earnings of up to 75 percent are exempt. Automobiles with up to $2,550 in equity are exempt. Up to $3,000 in the value of all other personal property can be exempt. Household furnishings, appliances, provisions, wearing apparel, and other personal effects are 100 percent exempt if they are ordinary and necessary. Up to $2,075 each for personal property used in the debtor's trade or business is exempt. California has an even more extensive list of possible exemptions, so go over your property list carefully with your attorney.

Colorado

You can get a homestead exemption of up to $45,000 for your home (which includes a mobile home). If you have more than $45,000 in equity and you file for Chapter 7 bankruptcy, the bankruptcy court could order your home sold to pay off your debtors. Only the state exemptions are allowed. Residents cannot use federal bankruptcy exemptions. Up to $25,000 in farm machinery, tools, and livestock can be exempt. Wages of up to 75 percent of your weekly, disposable earnings are exempt. One automobile up to $3,000 in value can be exempt (up to $6,000 if you are disabled). Up to $3,000 in the value of household furniture, furnishings, and appliances can be exempt. There's also an exemption of up to $1,500 for clothing, and for up to $1,000 for jewelry and watches. Tools of the trade are exempt up to $10,000, and there's a professional library exemption of up to $3,000. Up to $25,000 for the cash surrender value of an insurance policy is exempt. Personal books and family pictures are exempt up to $1,500.

Connecticut

You can get a homestead exemption of up to $75,000, which includes necessary apparel, bedding, foodstuffs, household furniture, appliances, tools, books, instruments, farm animals, and livestock feed (which are necessary to the debtor in the course of his or her occupation, profession, or farming operation). If you have higher equity in your home, you may want to consider using the federal exemption rules because that is an option in Connecticut. Talk with your attorney to find out which laws are better for you. You can exempt up to $1,500 for a motor vehicle. Up to an additional $1,000 in other property also can be exempt.

Delaware

You can get a homestead exemption of up to $50,000. If you have more than $50,000 in equity and you file for Chapter 7 bankruptcy, the bankruptcy court could order your home sold to pay off your debtors. Property held as tenancy by the entirety may be exempt against debts held by only one spouse. Only the state exemptions are allowed, so you can't use federal exemption rules. One automobile necessary for employment is exempt up to $15,000. Up to $25,000 on estate property can be exempt. There's also an exemption of up to $500 for personal property for the head of the household. Tools of the trade are exempt up to $15,000.

Florida

The homestead exemption is unlimited in Florida as long as your property does not exceed ½ acre in a municipality or 160 acres elsewhere. Thus, you can't lose your home if you're eligible for a Chapter 7 bankruptcy, as long as you agree to continue paying the mortgage. There's also an exemption of $1,000 for the equity you have in a motor vehicle. Property held as tenancy by the entirety may be exempt against debts held by only one spouse. The federal exemptions are not permitted as an alternative.

Georgia

You can get a homestead exemption of up to $10,000 ($20,000 if married). If you have more than $10,000 in equity and you file for Chapter 7 bankruptcy, the bankruptcy court could order your home sold to pay off your debtors. Only the state exemptions are allowed, so you can't use federal exemption rules. One automobile is exempt up to $3,500. There is also an exemption of up to $5,000 for household furnishings and goods, wearing apparel, appliances, books, animals, crops, or musical instruments that are primarily for personal family or household use, not to exceed $200 in value for each item and not to exceed $5,000 in aggregate value. Tools of the trade are exempt up to $1,500.

Hawaii

You can get a homestead exemption of up to $20,000 (up to $30,000 for a debtor who is married, head of household, or over 65) for property up to 1 acre in size. If you have more than $20,000 in equity and you file for Chapter 7 bankruptcy, the bankruptcy court could order your home sold to pay off your debtors. Property held as tenancy by the entirety may be exempt against debts held by only one spouse. You can choose to use the federal exemptions, so talk with your attorney to see which is better for you. One automobile is exempt up to $2,575. There is also an exemption of up to $1,000 for jewelry. Tools of the trade, a motor vehicle, and a commercial fishing boat needed for livelihood are exempt.

Idaho

You can get a homestead exemption of up to $50,000. If you have more than $50,000 in equity and you file for Chapter 7 bankruptcy, the bankruptcy court could order your home sold to pay off your debtors. Only the state exemptions are allowed, so you can't use federal exemption rules. Furnishings, one firearm, wearing apparel, household pets, books, musical instruments, family portraits, and heirlooms are limited to a value not exceeding $500 on any one item and not exceeding a total value of $5,000. Jewelry is exempt up to $1,000. A motor vehicle is exempt up to $3,000. Tools of the trade are exempt up to $1,500. You also have an $800 wildcard exemption that can be used in any category.

Illinois

You can get a homestead exemption of up to $7,500 per person. If two or more persons own property that is exempt, the maximum exemption is $15,000. That means that up to $15,000 of the equity in your home can be protected if two or more people own the home. If you have more than $15,000 in equity and you file for Chapter 7 bankruptcy, the bankruptcy court could order your home sold to pay off your debtors. You are entitled to up to $7,500 of the proceeds if the home is sold. Property held as tenancy by the entirety may be exempt against debts held by only one spouse. Only the state exemptions are allowed, so you can't use federal exemption rules. One automobile is exempt up to $1,200. There is also an exemption of up to $2,000 for wearing apparel, a Bible, schoolbooks, and family pictures of the debtor and dependents. Tools of the trade are exempt up to $750. If you've won a personal injury award, the first $7,500 is exempt.

Indiana

You can get a homestead exemption of up to $15,000. If you have more than $15,000 in equity and you file for Chapter 7 bankruptcy, the bankruptcy court could order your home sold to pay off your debtors. Only the state exemptions are allowed, so you can't use federal exemption rules. Property held as tenancy by the entirety may be exempt against debts held by only one spouse. Some other exemptions may include other real or tangible personal property up to $8,000. Professionally prescribed health aids and interest in retirement plan and medical care savings accounts are exempt.

Iowa

The homestead exemption is unlimited in Iowa, as long as the property does not exceed ½ acre in a town or city, or 40 acres elsewhere. Thus, you can't lose your home if you're eligible for a Chapter 7 bankruptcy, as long as you agree to continue paying the mortgage. Federal exemptions are not allowed. You can exempt wearing apparel and receptacles, musical instruments, and household goods and furnishings up to $7,000. Books, Bibles, and pictures are exempt up to $1,000. Jewelry can be exempt up to $2,000. A motor vehicle is exempt up to $7,000. Farm implements, livestock, and feed are exempt up to $10,000. Tools of the trade are exempt up to $10,000. Cash on hand, bank deposits, and other personal property are exempt up to $1,000.

Kansas

The homestead exemption is unlimited in Kansas as long as the property is less than 1 acre in a town or city or 160 acres elsewhere. Thus, you can't lose your home if you're eligible for a Chapter 7 bankruptcy, as long as you agree to continue paying the mortgage. Federal exemptions are not allowed. Personal property that is necessary to sustain the basic needs of the judgment debtor and his family are exempt. Jewelry is exempt up to $1,000. A motor vehicle is exempt up to $20,000. Tools of the trade are exempt up to $7,500.

Kentucky

You can get a homestead exemption of up to $5,000. If you have more than $5,000 in equity and you file for Chapter 7 bankruptcy, the bankruptcy court could order your home sold to pay off your debtors. You can use the rules for federal exemptions, so if you do have a lot of equity in your home, you may want to talk with your attorney about that option. There's a $3,000 exemption for tools, equipment, and livestock for farmers; otherwise, the exemption is $1,000 for tools of the trade. There's also a $1,000 exemption for household furniture, clothing, furnishings, and ornaments, and a $3,000 exemption for motor vehicles. In addition there's a $2,500 general exemption, but not more than $1,000 can be applied to any property, real or personal, tangible or intangible.

Louisiana

You can get a homestead exemption of up to $25,000 as long as your lot size does not exceed 5 acres in a town or city, or 200 acres elsewhere. If you have more than $25,000 in equity and you file for Chapter 7 bankruptcy, the bankruptcy court could order your home sold to pay off your debtors. Only the state exemptions are allowed, so you can't use federal exemption rules. You can also get a $7,500 exemption for a motor vehicle you use to go to and from work, and $5,000 for clothing and household items, musical instruments, domestic stocks, household pets, and wedding or engagement rings.

Maine

You can get a homestead exemption of up to $35,000 per person ($70,000 if married or a single person over age 60 or disabled, and $140,000 for a married couple over 60 or disabled). If you have more than $70,000 in equity and you file for Chapter 7 bankruptcy, the bankruptcy court could order your home sold to pay off your debtors. Only the state exemptions are allowed, so you can't use federal exemption rules. You can also get a $5,000 exemption for a motor vehicle and $5,000 for tools of the trade. Clothing, household furniture and furnishings, musical instruments, and other assets that are held primarily for the personal family or household use of the debtor or his dependents are exempt, provided that the value does not exceed $200 for each item.

Maryland

The state has no homestead exemption, but property held as tenancy by the entirety is exempt if only one spouse holds the debts. If you are not protected by the tenancy by the entirety rule, the bankruptcy court could order your home sold to pay off your debtors. Only the state exemptions are allowed, so you can't use federal exemption rules. You can also get a $1,200 exemption for a motor vehicle and $750 for tools of the trade. There's a $2,500 exemption for household furnishings and goods, clothing, appliances, books, animals, crops, and musical instruments. There's an exemption for jewelry up to $500 and no exemption limit on health aids.

Massachusetts

You can get a homestead exemption of up to $500,000. If you have more than $500,000 in equity and you file for Chapter 7 bankruptcy, the bankruptcy court could order your home sold to pay off your debtors. You can use state or federal exemptions, but since state homestead exemptions are more generous, you'll likely want to file using state rules. Property held as tenancy by the entirety may be exempt against debts held by only one spouse. You can also get a $700 exemption for a motor vehicle and $500 for tools of the trade. There's a $3,000 exemption for household goods. There's an exemption for a bank account up to $500, and there's no exemption limit on wearing apparel.

Michigan

You can get a homestead exemption of up to $31,900 ($47,825 if over age 65 or disabled) as long as the lot size is no more than 1 lot in a town, city, or village, or 40 acres elsewhere. If you have more than $31,900 in equity and you file for Chapter 7 bankruptcy, the bankruptcy court could order your home sold to pay off your debtors. Property held as tenancy by the entirety may be exempt against debts held by only one spouse. There's a $1,000 exemption for tools of the trade. There's also a $3,200 exemption for household goods and a $2,950 exemption for motor vehicles. There's an exemption of up to $525 for household pets, and $525 for one computer and accessories. Church pew, slip, seat for entire family up to $525 is exempt. There's also a $2,125 exemption for crops, farm animals, and feed.

Minnesota

You can get a homestead exemption of up to $200,000 (up to $500,000 for agricultural property) as long as the lot size does not exceed ½ acre in a city or 160 acres elsewhere. If you have more than $200,000 in equity and you file for Chapter 7 bankruptcy, the bankruptcy court could order your home sold to pay off your debtors. You can use state or federal exemptions, but since state homestead exemptions are more generous, you'll likely want to file using state rules. You can also get a $3,800 exemption for a motor vehicle (if modified for the disabled, up to $38,000) and $9,500 for tools of the trade (up to $13,000 for farming equipment). There's an $8,550 exemption for household furniture.

Mississippi

You can get a homestead exemption of up to $75,000, but the lot size cannot exceed 160 acres. If you have more than $75,000 in equity and you file for Chapter 7 bankruptcy, the bankruptcy court could order your home sold to pay off your debtors. Only the state exemptions are allowed, so you can't use federal exemption rules. There's also a $10,000 exemption for tangible personal property, including household goods (excluding art, antiques, electronic equipment other than one television and one radio, and jewelry other than wedding rings), clothing, motor vehicles, trade implements, health aids, and cash.

Missouri

You can get a homestead exemption of up to $15,000 per person (up to $5,000 for a mobile home used as a residence). If you have more than $15,000 in equity and you file for Chapter 7 bankruptcy, the bankruptcy court could order your home sold to pay off your debtors. Only the state exemptions are allowed, so you can't use federal exemption rules. Property held as tenancy by the entirety may be exempt against debts held by only one spouse. You can also get a $3,000 exemption for a motor vehicle and $3,000 for household furnishings, household goods, wearing apparel, appliances, books, animals, crops, or musical instruments that are held primarily for the use of the debtor and dependents. There's a $500 exemption for jewelry and a $1,500 exemption for a wedding ring. There's no limit on professional health aids for the debtor or dependents. Up to $3,000 is exempt for tools of the trade.

Montana

You can get a homestead exemption of up to $100,000 per person ($200,000 if filing jointly). If you have more than $200,000 in equity and you file for Chapter 7 bankruptcy, the bankruptcy court could order your home sold to pay off your debtors. Only the state exemptions are allowed. You can also get a $2,500 exemption for a motor vehicle and $750 for tools of the trade. There's a $4,500 exemption for household furnishings and goods, appliances, jewelry, wearing apparel, books, firearms and other sporting goods, animals, feed, crops, and musical instruments to the extent of a value not exceeding $600 in any item or $4,500. There's an exemption for tools of the trade up to $3,000, and there's no exemption limit on health aids.

Nebraska

You can get a homestead exemption of up to $12,500 as long as your property does not exceed 2 lots in a city or village or 160 acres elsewhere. If you have more than $12,500 in equity and you file for Chapter 7 bankruptcy, the bankruptcy court could order your home sold to pay off your debtors. Only the state exemptions are allowed, so you can't use federal exemption rules. There's also a $1,500 exemption for wearing apparel and household furniture and furnishings. You can get an exemption for books, tools of the trade, and/or automobiles, up to an aggregate fair market value of 2,400. There's also a wildcard exemption of up to $2,500 for personal property.

Nevada

You can get a homestead exemption of up to $350,000. If you have more than $350,000 in equity and you file for Chapter 7 bankruptcy, the bankruptcy court could order your home sold to pay off your debtors. Only the state exemptions are allowed, so you can't use federal exemption rules. There's also a $5,000 exemption for private libraries and a $12,000 exemption for all family pictures and keepsakes, necessary household goods, and yard equipment. You can exempt up to $4,500 for farm trucks, farm stock, farm tools, farm equipment, supplies, and seed; up to $4,500 for a cabin or dwelling of a miner or prospector, his cars, and implements and appliances necessary for carrying on any mining operations and his mining claim actually worked by the debtor up to $15,000 in value. There's no limit on prosthesis or equipment prescribed by a physician or dentist. You can exempt up to $10,000 for tools of the trade.

New Hampshire

You can get a homestead exemption of up to $100,000. If you have more than $100,000 in equity and you file for Chapter 7 bankruptcy, the bankruptcy court could order your home sold to pay off your debtors. Only the state exemptions are allowed, so you can't use federal exemption rules. There's no limit on wearing apparel or comfortable beds, bedsteads, and bedding necessary for the debtor, his wife, and children. There's a $3,500 exemption on household furniture, and up to $800 on Bibles, schoolbooks, and a library. Some farm animals are exempt, including one hog and one pig, and the pork of the same when slaughtered; six sheep, and the fleeces of the same; one cow; a yoke of oxen or a horse, when required for farming or teaming purposes or other actual use; hay not exceeding 4 tons; and domestic fowls not exceeding $300 in value. You can get an exemption of up to $4,000 for a motor vehicle, up to $500 for jewelry, and up to $5,000 for tools of the trade.

New Jersey

There's no homestead exemption, but you can use federal exemptions. The survivorship interest of a spouse for property held as tenancy by the entirety may be exempt against debts held by only one spouse. You can get up to $1,000 for goods and chattels, shares of stock or interests in any corporation, and personal property of every kind; there's another $1,000 exemption for household goods and furniture. There's no limit on wearing apparel that can be exempt.

New Mexico

You can get a homestead exemption of up to $30,000. If you have more than $30,000 in equity and you file for Chapter 7 bankruptcy, the bankruptcy court could order your home sold to pay off your debtors. You can use state or federal exemptions, so you may want to talk with your attorney about which is best for you. If you don't have a home, you can claim an exemption up to $2,000 for real or personal property in lieu of a homestead exemption. You can also get a $4,000 exemption for a motor vehicle and $1,500 for tools of the trade. There's a $500 exemption for personal items and $2,500 for jewelry.

New York

You can get a homestead exemption of up to $50,000 per person ($100,000 for a married couple). If you have more than $100,000 in equity and you file for Chapter 7 bankruptcy, the bankruptcy court could order your home sold to pay off your debtors. Only the state exemptions are allowed. You can also get a $2,400 exemption for a motor vehicle and $5,000 for tools of the trade. There's an exemption of up to $5,000 for the family Bible, family pictures, and schoolbooks; $450 for household pets; $5,000 for wearing apparel, household furniture, one mechanical or gas or electric refrigerator, one radio receiver, one television set, crockery, tableware, and cooking utensils necessary; and up to $5,000 for a wedding ring.

North Carolina

You can get a homestead exemption of up to $18,500 per person ($37,000 for a married couple). If you have more than $37,000 in equity and you file for Chapter 7 bankruptcy, the bankruptcy court could order your home sold to pay off your debtors. Property held as tenancy by the entirety may be exempt against debts held by only one spouse. Only the state exemptions are allowed. You can also get a $3,500 exemption for a motor vehicle and $2,000 for tools of the trade. There's an exemption of up to $5,000 for household goods, wearing apparel, appliances, books, animals, crops, or musical instruments that are held primarily for personal, family, or household use, up to $5,000 for the debtor plus $1,000 for each dependent, but not to exceed $4,000 total for the dependents.

North Dakota

You can get a homestead exemption of up to $80,000. If you have more than $80,000 in equity and you file for Chapter 7 bankruptcy, the bankruptcy court could order your home sold to pay off your debtors. Only the state exemptions are allowed, so you can't use federal exemption rules. There's no limit on the exemption for wearing apparel, family pictures, or provisions for the debtor and his family necessary for one year's supply of crops and grain (not to exceed 160 acres of land). A house trailer or mobile home occupied as a residence by the debtor is exempt. Up to $5,000 for a head of household or $2,500 for a single person can be exempt for personal property, any goods, chattels, merchandise, money, and other personal property. You can exempt up to $1,200 for a motor vehicle. You can choose up to a $7,500 exemption in lieu of a homestead exemption. Alternative exemptions include miscellaneous books and musical instruments, not to exceed $1,500 in value; household and kitchen furniture, not to exceed $1,000 in value; livestock and farm implements, not to exceed $4,500 in value; tools and implements of any mechanic and stock in trade, not to exceed $1,000 in value; and library and instruments of any profession, not to exceed $1,000 in value.

Ohio

You can get a homestead exemption of up to $5,000. If you have more than $5,000 in equity and you file for Chapter 7 bankruptcy, the bankruptcy court could order your home sold to pay off your debtors. Only the state exemptions are allowed, so you can't take use federal exemption rules. Property held as tenancy by the entirety may be exempt against debts held by only one spouse. You can exempt up to $400 in cash. If claiming a homestead exemption, household goods and furnishings can be exempt to $200 each, up to a total of $1,500. If not claiming a homestead exemption, household goods and furnishings can be exempt to a maximum of $200 each, up to a total of $2,000. You can exempt up to $1,500 in jewelry if you're claiming a homestead exemption and up to $2,000 if you're not claiming a homestead exemption. You can exempt up to $1,000 for a motor vehicle and up to $750 for tools of the trade. You can also exempt up to $1,500 of personal property as a wildcard.

Oklahoma

You can exempt real property or a manufactured home to unlimited value as long as the property does not exceed ¼ acre. If property exceeds ¼ acre, you may claim $10,000 on 1 acre in a city, town, or village, or 160 acres elsewhere. (You don't need to occupy a homestead to claim it as exempt, as long as you don't acquire another homestead.) Household and kitchen furniture held primarily for personal, family, or household use are exempt, as are books, portraits, and pictures that are held primarily for personal, family, or household use. You can exempt wedding and anniversary rings up to $3,000. You can exempt implements of husbandry necessary to farm the homestead, up to $10,000. Wearing apparel is exempt up to $4,000, tools of the trade up to $5,000, and motor vehicles up to $7,500. Professionally prescribed health aids are exempt. You can also exempt up to 5 milk cows and their calves under 6 months old; 100 chickens; 2 horses and 2 bridles and 2 saddles; 10 hogs; 20 head of sheep; all provisions and forage on hand, or growing for home consumption, and for the use of exempt stock for one year.

Oregon

You can get a homestead exemption of up to $30,000 per person ($39,600 if two or more members of a household are debtors) as long as the property does not include more than one block in a town or city or 160 acres elsewhere. If you have more than $39,600 in equity and you file for Chapter 7 bankruptcy, the bankruptcy court could order your home sold to pay off your debtors. Only the state exemptions are allowed. If you own a mobile home, you can get an exemption of up to $23,000 for a mobile home and lot in lieu of a homestead exemption ($30,000 if more than one owner owes the debt). If you have a mobile home but don't own a lot, you can get an exemption of up to $20,000 ($27,0000 if more than one owner owes the debt) in lieu of a homestead exemption. You can get an exemption of up to $600 for books, pictures, and musical instruments; up to $1,800 for each spouse for wearing apparel, jewelry, and other personal items; up to $1,000 for domestic animals and poultry kept for family use; up to $3,000 for household goods, furniture, radios, a television set, and utensils; up to $3,000 for a motor vehicle; up to $1,000 for a rifle, shotgun, or one pistol; and up to $3,000 for tools of the trade. Professionally prescribed health aids for the debtor or a dependent of the debtor are exempt.

Pennsylvania

There's no homestead exemption, but you are allowed to use the federal homestead exemption. Property held as tenancy by the entirety may be exempt against debts held by only one spouse. A debtor may claim exemption for wearing apparel; Bibles and schoolbooks; sewing machines belonging to seamstresses or used and owned by private families, but not including sewing machines kept for sale or hire; and uniforms and accouterments.

Rhode Island

You can get a homestead exemption of up to $300,000. If you have more than $300,000 in equity and you file for Chapter 7 bankruptcy, the bankruptcy court could order your home sold to pay off your debtors. Property held as tenancy by the entirety may be exempt against debts held by only one spouse. You can use state or federal exemptions, but since state homestead exemptions are more generous, you likely will want to file using state rules. You can also get a $10,000 exemption for a motor vehicle and $1,200 for tools of the trade. There's an $8,600 exemption for household furniture and family stores, including beds and bedding. There's also an exemption for jewelry up to $1,000.

South Carolina

You can get a homestead exemption of up to $50,000 per debtor (up to $100,000 per residence). If you have more than $100,000 in equity and you file for Chapter 7 bankruptcy, the bankruptcy court could order your home sold to pay off your debtors. You can use only state exemptions. If you don't have a homestead, in lieu of the homestead exemption, you can exempt up to $1,000 for cash and liquid assets. You can also get a $1,200 exemption for a motor vehicle and $750 for tools of the trade. There's a $2,500 exemption for household furnishings and goods, clothing, appliances, books, animals, crops, and musical instruments. There's also an exemption for jewelry up to $500. All health aids are exempt.

South Dakota

You can get an unlimited homestead exemption on property as long as your lot size does not exceed 1 acre in a town or 160 acres elsewhere. Only state exemptions are allowed. You can exempt up to $4,000 for goods, chattels, merchandise, money, or other personal property. There's an additional exemption for personal property or cash of up to $6,000 for a head of household or $4,000 for a single person. You can also exempt up to $200 of miscellaneous books and musical instruments, and up to $1,250 of farm equipment.

Tennessee

You can get a homestead exemption of up to $5,000 ($7,500 for joint owners, $12,500 if 62 or older, $20,000 if 62 or older and married, and $25,000 if both spouses are 62 or older). If you have more than $5,000 in equity and you file for Chapter 7 bankruptcy, the bankruptcy court could order your home sold to pay off your debtors. Property held as tenancy by the entirety may be exempt against debts held by only one spouse. Only state exemptions are allowed. You can exempt up to $4,000 of money and funds on deposit with a bank or other financial institution. You can get an exemption of up to $1,900 for tools of the trade. You get an absolute exemption for all necessary wearing apparel for the actual use of the debtor and his or her family, the trunks or receptacles necessary to contain family portraits and pictures, and the family Bible and schoolbooks.

Texas

There's no limit on the amount of homestead exemption you can claim, as long as your lot size is no more than 10 acres in a town or city or 100 acres elsewhere (200 acres for families). You can get an exemption of up to $30,000 (up to $60,000 for a family) for personal property. You can use either state or federal exemptions, but since there's no limit on your homestead exemption, you'll likely be better off choosing to use the state exemption laws.

Utah

You can get a homestead exemption of up to $20,000. If you have more than $20,000 in equity and you file for Chapter 7 bankruptcy, the bankruptcy court could order your home sold to pay off your debtors. Only state exemptions are allowed. There's no limit on the amount you can exempt for health aids reasonably necessary to enable the debtor or a dependent to work or sustain health. You can exempt up to $2,500 for a motor vehicle. You can exempt one clothes washer and dryer, one refrigerator, one freezer, one stove, one microwave oven, one sewing machine, all carpets in use, provisions sufficient for 12 months actually provided for individual or family use, all wearing apparel (not including jewelry or furs), all beds and bedding, and all works of art depicting the debtor or the debtor and his resident family, or produced by the debtor or the debtor and his resident family, except works of art held by the debtor as part of a trade or business. You can exempt up to $500 for sofas, chairs, and related furnishings; $500 for dining and kitchen tables and chairs; up to $500 for animals, books, and musical instruments; and up to $500 for heirlooms or other items of particular sentimental value.

Vermont

You can get a homestead exemption of up to $75,000. If you have more than $75,000 in equity and you file for Chapter 7 bankruptcy, the bankruptcy court could order your home sold to pay off your debtors. Property held as tenancy by the entirety may be exempt against debts held by only one spouse. You can use state or federal exemptions. You may want to discuss using federal instead of state exemptions with your attorney. You can get a $2,500 exemption for a motor vehicle and $5,000 for tools of the trade. You can get up to a $5,000 exemption for household furnishings, goods or appliances, books, wearing apparel, animals, crops, or musical instruments that are held primarily for personal, family, or household use of the debtor or his dependents. There's up to a $5,000 exemption for growing crops. You can also exempt 1 cooking stove; appliances needed for heating; 1 refrigerator; 1 freezer; 1 water heater; sewing machines; 10 cords of firewood; 5 tons of coal or 500 gallons of oil; 500 gallons of bottled gas; 1 cow; 2 goats; 10 sheep; 10 chickens; feed sufficient to keep the cow, goats, sheep, or chickens through one winter; 3 swarms of bees and their hives, with their produce in honey; 1 yoke of oxen or steers, or 2 horses kept and used for team work; 2 harnesses, 2 halters, 2 chains, 1 plow, and 1 ox yoke; and bank account deposits not to exceed $700 in value. You can exempt jewelry up to $500. You can exempt all professionally prescribed health aids for the debtor or his or her dependents.

Virginia

You can get a homestead exemption of up to $5,000 (you can get an additional exemption of $500 for each dependent, and there's an additional $2,500 for a disabled veteran). If you have more than $5,000 in equity and you file for Chapter 7 bankruptcy, the bankruptcy court could order your home sold to pay off your debtors. Property held as tenancy by the entirety may be exempt against debts held by only one spouse. Only state exemptions are allowed. You can exempt up to $2,000 for a motor vehicle. There's a homestead allowance for a

surviving spouse of up to $15,000. You can get exemptions of up to
$1,000 on wearing apparel; up to $5,000 on wedding and engagement
rings, family portraits, and heirlooms; up to $5,000 for household fur-
niture; up to $15,000 for exempt property of someone who died; up
to $4,000 on farmers' equipment; and up to $10,000 for tools of the
trade.

Washington

You can get a homestead exemption of up to $40,000. If you have
more than $40,000 in equity and you file for Chapter 7 bankruptcy,
the bankruptcy court could order your home sold to pay off your
debtors. You can use state or federal homestead exemption rules, so
talk with your attorney about which ones would be better for you.
If you do use state rules, you also get exemptions of up to $1,000 for
wearing apparel; up to $1,500 for furs, jewelry, and personal ornaments
for any individual; private libraries; up to $1,500 for family pictures
and keepsakes; up to $2,700 for household goods, appliances, furniture,
and home and yard equipment; and up to $2,000 for other personal
property. You can also get an exemption of $2,500 for a motor vehi-
cle (up to $5,000 for two motor vehicles) and up to $100 in cash or
bank accounts. You can get exemptions of up to $5,000 for tools of the
trade and up to $2,500 for professional library, office furniture, office
equipment, and supplies.

Washington, D.C.

Although the District of Columbia does not call it a homestead
exemption, it does provide an unlimited exemption for a personal
residence. Property held as tenancy by the entirety may be exempt
against debts held by only one spouse. You can use the federal
exemption laws. If you do use the D.C. laws, you can exempt wearing apparel not exceeding $300 per person in the household; up to
$425 for beds, bedding, household furniture and furnishings, sewing
machines, radios, stoves, and cooking utensils; up to $200 in mechan-
ics' tools (non–head of family); up to $400 for family pictures and

a library; up to $300 for a library, office furniture, and implements of a professional man or artist; up to $2,575 for a motor vehicle; up to $400 for all family pictures and all family library materials; up to $1,625 for tools of the trade; and up to $850 for aggregate interest in any property.

You can exempt up to a total of $8,625 for household furnishings, appliances, and wearing apparel.

West Virginia

You can get a homestead exemption of up to $25,000. If you have more than $25,000 in equity and you file for Chapter 7 bankruptcy, the bankruptcy court could order your home sold to pay off your debtors. Only state exemptions are allowed. You can get an exemption of up to $1,000 for personal property and up to $8,000 for household furnishings, goods, wearing apparel, appliances, books, animals, crops, or musical instruments that are held primarily for personal, family, or household use of the debtor or a dependent of the debtor, not to exceed $400 in value for any particular item and not to exceed $8,000 in total value. You can get an exemption of up to $1,000 for jewelry held primarily for personal, family, or household use of the debtor or his or her dependents. All professionally prescribed health aids for the debtor or a dependent are exempt. There's an exemption of up to $2,400 for a motor vehicle and up to $1,500 for tools of the trade.

Wisconsin

You can get a homestead exemption of up to $40,000. If you have more than $40,000 in equity and you file for Chapter 7 bankruptcy, the bankruptcy court could order your home sold to pay off your debtors. Property held as tenancy by the entirety may be exempt against debts held by only one spouse. You can use state or federal exemptions, so you should talk with your attorney to find out which ones will be better for you to use. If you do use state rules, in addition to the homestead exemption, you can get an exemption of up to

$5,000 in consumer goods, up to $5,000 in homestead furnishings, up to $1,200 in motor vehicles, up to $1,000 in deposit accounts, and up to $7,500 in tools of the trade.

Wyoming

The homestead may be a house and lot or a farm consisting of any number of acres, up to $10,000. If you own a house trailer or other moveable home that is being used as a residence, up to $6,000 can be exempt. If you have more than $10,000 in equity and you file for Chapter 7 bankruptcy, the bankruptcy court could order your home sold to pay off your debtors. Property held as tenancy by the entirety may be exempt against debts held by only one spouse. Only state exemption laws can be used. Other exemptions include up to $1,000 for wearing apparel, including wedding rings: up to $2,000 for a family Bible, pictures, and schoolbooks; a lot in any cemetery or burial ground; furniture, bedding, provisions, and other household articles of any kind or character that the debtor may select; and up to $2,000 for a library, instruments, and implements of any professional person. You can exempt up to $2,000 for a motor vehicle and up to $2,000 for tools of the trade.

Index

Numbers

Q-R

S

U-V

W-X-Y-Z